Amazing Secrets To Making The Most of Your Teenage Years

Grace U. Anighoro

Hey Girl!
Amazing Secrets To Making
The Most of Your Teenage Years

First published in the United Kingdom in 2020
by The Kingdom Publications

Book design: Adeola Disu
The Kingdom Publications
info@thekingdompublications.com

Printed in the United Kingdom

Dear Amelia
Merry christmas,
I Love You
Mum
Dec 2020

DEDICATION

This book is dedicated to YOU, a girl born to rock her world.
A girl, who is ready to take her destiny in her hands and
live to her full potential.

I believe in you.

CONTENTS

FOREWORD BY
DR. SUNDAY ADELAJA

This book is the truth. For anyone who would get a hold of this book, I want to tell you that this is the truth that the world won't tell you, this is the truth that your age mates won't tell you, this is the truth that your teachers won't tell you. The truths in this book are even some that your parents would not be comfortable telling you about. This book should become the teenage girl's Bible of sorts.

It is not just a book, but a guidebook for life. Grace has done a great great job by putting this book together. All parents are supposed to get this book for their girl child. All teenage girls are supposed to have it by their bed. This book is a book that will protect and guide any teenager from the pitfalls of life. I am going to give this book to my girls as a must read. So much sorrow, so much tears could be prevented, if only people would read this book.

I actually feel that it is not enough to just read it, but it needs to be studied. It would teach you to value your teenage years, and to invest your life in the right things. It will prevent your life from being wasted and lead you in the right direction of fulfillment.

This book is all about love. The love from which it is written is glaring from every page in the book. It is only a heart of love that can produce this kind of book. I would like to say that this book should be given and recommended to everyone you know. They will come back and thank you for it.

Meanwhile I would like to say thank you very much to Grace for being a blessing for the next generation."

Much love,

Sunday Adelaja

Founder, Senior Pastor, Embassy of God Church, Kiev, Ukraine

ACKNOWLEDGMENTS

I strongly believe in the education and empowerment of the girl child. We owe it to the next generation to equip them with the right knowledge and skills that will help them achieve their full potential. No girl should be ignorant. No girl should suffer pain. No girl deserves to be abused.

My burden for equipping and supporting the girl child led me to start a club for girls known as; The Marvellous Girls Club (TMGC) (Ltd). This book is written as a result t of my work with the girls in my community over the last three years. It is an attempt to pour my heart out to every girl all over the world who will read this book to develop themselves and become a strong woman tomorrow.

I am particularly grateful to my dear mentor Dr Sunday Adelaja, whose teachings awakened me to my purpose. I started living again when I heard your teachings. Everything in me came alive and now I can say I am not just existing but I am truly alive. I wouldn't start a club or be writing a book if not for your mentorship and tutelage that gave me the courage and the boldness to live in my purpose.

To my dear husband - Odafe Anighoro, I never would be able to do any of this without your strong support, understanding, sacrifice and encouragement. You make it so easy to be a wife. I love you so dearly and I'm so blessed that you are with me on this journey.

To my children Ruky and Runor, I love you both so much. Thank you for your understanding and your sacrifice. I know how much you want to stay home sometimes but you still go along with me to the club to support me. You show such maturity and try to leave me alone when you know I'm busy reading or writing. Thank you, Runor Faith, my angel helper, for always trying to help your brother as much as you can when I'm not there.

To all at the Release Writing Programme. My connection with you is truly divine. Who would have thought I would be able to complete a book in such a short time? My thanks and appreciation go to Naima B Robert, Hend Hegazi and the entire editorial team.

You guys are amazing. Your push, encouragement, criticism and amazing support have made this book possible! May Allah's blessing be on you all.

To my talented and hardworking sister and friend, Adeola Disu. Thank you so much for your help and support. There's nothing I would have wanted more than to have you living close to me. Maybe we can be neighbours someday. Thank you for being so accommodating and so helpful with the designing of the book cover and all. You are always helping out with my promotional flyers and events flyers anytime I need them. I truly appreciate you. May God strengthen and keep you in good health and give you length of days.

INTRODUCTION

Hey, girl!

This book is for the young tween, teen or young adult who is interested in making the most of her life. You seek to maximise your time at this crucial stage of your growth so as not to end up regretting in the future. You want to know and focus on the things that are truly important so that you can look back and say, 'Yes! My teenage years were not a waste.'

That was how it was for me.

My memories of being a teenager are, for the most part, exciting. It was challenging and confusing at times, of course, but it was one of the best seasons of my life. Not because I had everything I wanted, no! It was because I was able to learn essential lessons that prepared me for adulthood. I was able to learn from the wisdom and mistakes of others and have a dream for how I wanted my life to go. I could have learnt even more to prepare me for adulthood, but resources were scarce back then. You are living at a time when information and resources are readily available. You don't have an excuse. Being a teenager can be tough, especially with school-work, assignments and examinations, and friends and family pressures. But it doesn't have to be tough if you apply the ideas I am going to write about in this book.

I am so excited to be writing this book for you. I was a young girl just like you once. Every woman, wife, mother, aunt and niece is first a girl. No matter how old we get in life, that girl is still very much alive in us

You are a girl!

A girl - innocent and sweet.

A girl - young and free.

A girl - filled with so many hopes and dreams.

A girl - born for a purpose.

A girl - packaged with so much potential.

A girl- born to rock her world.

I grew up in a family of girls. My mother had five sisters herself. In my family, we were six females and three males. I had step-siblings and cousins who were mostly girls. When it was time to go to secondary school, I attended an all-girls school too. I guess because I had girls all around me, I experienced a time in my life when I didn't want to be one.

The society I was in didn't have a high regard for girls. What I observed around me formed my perception of girls. Girls were, more often than not, treated as weak and inferior to boys. Sadly, this has not changed much as gender bias is still very prevalent in many communities today. I didn't want to be considered weak or inferior to a boy. I didn't want to be denied any privileges merely for being a girl.

Despite all the fun activities going on in secondary school, there were also some sad times too. For some girls, these were troublesome years. A lot of girls were involved in unacceptable behaviour, and we also had some teachers that were not nice.

Maybe you are about to start secondary school, are in secondary school, or you may have left secondary school already.

What are your own experiences at school?

What kind of school do you attend? Is it a single-sex school or a mixed school?

Are you having fun at school or is school a pain?

I realise that, for many, school is a pain these days.

Although times have changed, a lot of the issues that I experienced when I was a student are still prevalent today. I guess I can say that girls will always be girls.

When I was young, some girls had a difficult time at home too. Some were rude and stubborn and always argued with their parents. For most girls, the frustration of not having what others had impacted their confidence and self–esteem. A classmate of ours was upset because she didn't get her way with her parents. She took some pills to end her life but survived. She had to go to a hospital. We lost another classmate to sickle cell disease.

How are things for you at home?

Do you always get everything you want?

Do you feel that your parents understand you?

It could be that you also know a girl who is experiencing difficulties with challenging behaviour. Or maybe you know a girl with a health issue. We all come from different backgrounds, and our experiences are different.

My experience of secondary school was filled with responsibilities and activities. I was an active student. I participated in extracurricular activities, end of year school dances, and Independence Day celebrations. I joined the school Press Club as a sports reporter in my second year at secondary school. I became the president of the Press Club soon after, a position I held until I left secondary school three years later. I also had opportunities to represent my school in debates and quiz competitions, both locally and interstate. I was also actively involved in sports and was a member of the school hockey team.

As president of the press club, I took on the responsibility for social activities in school. I was involved in organising drama shows and discos. I was privileged to have a school principal who supported my activities in the school and was proud of me. I was also given recognition from my school and my local district as one of two of the best-behaved students in the school.

Despite all of these, I see now that, for many of us girls, there was no understanding of self, of our value and worth. At school, our teachers paid more attention to our academic abilities. At home, our parents just wanted us to get good grades, go to college, pick a good career, get married and have children.

There was hardly any preparation for the realities of life, and as a result of this, we lacked the skills needed to live a truly fulfilling life. We studied because our parents wanted us to and some pursued careers prescribed by their parents. Many did not even have a dream of their future. Some girls from my class got married and didn't pursue any further education. There was no sense of purpose and potential was wasted and never realised as a result of cultural and societal restrictions. Many who went on to pursue further education and had fantastic careers could not deal with the other realities and challenges that life threw at them. They soon began to realise that there was more to life than a good career.

> *"A child educated ONLY at school is an uneducated child"*
> *– George Santayana.[1]*

You are at the most crucial time of your life. What you do, coupled with the choices you make at this phase of your life, will go a long way to determining how fulfilling and successful your life will be.

Hey. girl! Life is a challenge. Life is transient. Life is also an opportunity! If you do not have the right values and don't make the right choices now, you can never do a rewind. It doesn't matter what it is you may be dealing with right now; you can still become what I call a Marvellous Girl.

Who is this Marvellous Girl?

She is the girl who lays a good foundation for her life as a teenager. She has a dream and starts working towards her dream *now*. She is a happy, bold, strong and confident teenager. It doesn't matter what her background is or if she's from a wealthy or low-income family. As a Marvellous Girl, you can be anything you want to be. You were born for a purpose! You were born to do great things. You have to make the most of your time now. There is no limit to the things you can do if you put your mind to it.

In this book, I will be sharing principles and values that will help you navigate through life. These are the tools you need to develop yourself as you journey into adulthood.

While growing up as a teenager, life is still made out to look as though your greatest achievements should be to get an education, get a good job, get married and have children. However, there *is* more to life. While getting an education is essential, more important is how prepared you are for life and its challenges.

It may seem unfair but your ability to pull through and live a fulfilling life will depend a lot on how prepared you are for your journey into adulthood. This book will equip you with the skills you need to prepare for the challenges and the tests of life. You can be happy and fulfilled despite the problems that may come your way. You don't need to live a life of pain and regret. You don't have to live in anxiety and depression. You don't have to be confused, seeking love and acceptance in the wrong places. Yes, you will make mistakes, but you don't have to allow those mistakes to define you. Better still, you can learn from the mistakes of others, so you don't have to repeat them.

In this book, you will discover yourself and your true identity. You will learn to recognise your true worth and value. You will know why having a dream and living a life of focus is crucial. You will learn the importance of delayed gratification and its benefits. This book will equip you with the values you need to make the right choices in life. You will learn how to cultivate meaningful and respectful relationships. You will learn how to maximise your potential. Above all, this book will guide you into living an intentional and purposeful life as a teen and young adult where you maximise your time.

CHAPTER 1

WHY AM I PASSIONATE ABOUT SUPPORTING TEENAGE GIRLS?

Many teenagers are under pressure nowadays, especially as a result of social media. The pressure to be perfect and to achieve is becoming worse. Some girls are self-harming and suffering from poor mental health, while some are becoming victims of domestic abuse and cyber-bullying. How can you overcome all of these pressures?

As we go along in this book, I will be sharing some stories and experiences that have helped to shape my life with you. I hope that these examples will guide you to make the most of your teenage years. I also hope that they will help you to use your time well and develop the correct values in life so as not to become part of the negative statistics.

There were things I saw among girls when I was growing up. As the president of the Press Club—the school watchdog at the time—there were lots of stories I heard involving girls and what they were up to. Some I was not able to publish. When I did report some of the stories to the school principal, I got into trouble because of how grievous each report was. One time, my classmates took revenge on me—they took my school bag with all my books inside. It was not a pleasant experience.

In secondary school, there were cases of girls suddenly dropping out because they fell pregnant at fourteen, fifteen or sixteen. It was sad news anytime someone stopped attending school as a result of being pregnant. And, of course, there were the cliques. These were the girls who felt they were better than others. My school was a day and boarding school. I remember the quarrels and fights that usually occurred between the two groups. There were internal fights too. I remember girls fighting over boys to the extent of hurting each other. Most of the arguments didn't even make any sense. A girl almost lost her ear in a row over a boy!

The things I saw and experienced are what made me passionate about teenage girls. When I was graduating secondary school, I felt sad for the younger students just coming into school and for the way the school system was changing. I could see that many young ones were not going to have the guidance and opportunities that I had enjoyed and I saw how necessary it was for those young ones to have mentors who would help them stay focused in order to finish secondary school successfully. But with the new changes, the younger students wouldn't have this. I felt the pull in my heart, but I couldn't do anything about it. My focus was on furthering my education and moving on to university.

University is a place of freedom. Parents don't watch over you. Teachers don't supervise you directly as they do in primary school and secondary school. It goes like this: when you are in primary school, you have close contact with your teachers, and they watch over you. In secondary school, the teachers are there, but there is a bit of freedom as they do not supervise you as much. They are focused on teaching you to get good grades. At university, you go and attend your lectures, or you may choose not to. Your lecturer rarely has any contact with you except for assignments and course work. So, your freedom here is greater, and this is your pathway to living independently from your family.

I could see that a lot of girls were getting into trouble both academically and socially because they could not handle this level of freedom. They did not have the maturity to deal with it. While some were intelligent and focused on pursuing their course of studies, others who *were* also smart girls became distracted. There were stories of abuse, rape and abortions. Some girls lost their lives simply for being at the wrong place at the wrong time.

Reports from Public Health England state that teenage mothers are more likely than other young people to not be pursuing education, employment or training; and by the age of 30 are 22% more likely to be living in poverty than mothers giving birth aged 24 or over. Fathers under 30 are twice as likely to be unemployed as their older counterparts, even after taking into account deprivation such as poverty. A recent analysis of the Next Steps data shows that some of these poor outcomes, notably poor mental health, are also experienced by parents under 25. [2]

Recent statistics from the BBC (British Broadcasting Commission) state that many teenagers in Britain are going through depression[3]. "There has been a rise in suicide rates among girls between the ages of ten to fourteen years," states a recent report by CNN (Cable News Network).[4]

Now that I am an adult, I hear from many women about the regrets they have due to poor choices. While they look good on the outside, on the inside, they are hurting. Some have gone through so many painful and stressful experiences that it is heart-breaking. Some ladies today are experiencing abuse and dealing with domestic violence. Some are struggling through life just because they got their priorities wrong while they were younger. Some are poor because they did not develop themselves and acquire the skills they needed to be able to work. Even those that have gone on to achieve a good education and good careers have become so subdued by life challenges that their mental health has been dramatically affected.

No girl should go through a life of pain and struggles. You should not go to sleep at night crying secret tears and wetting your pillows. You should not be ignorant of the realities of life and its challenges. That is why you must keep reading this book.

I want you to have the right values to enable you to make the right choices in life.

I want you to recognise your worth and your benefits.

I want you to be able to maximise your potential.

I want you to pursue and fulfil the purpose of why you are here on planet Earth.

> *"Don't live your life regretting yesterday. Live your life so tomorrow you won't regret today."*
> *– Catherine Pulsifer*[5]

To help me in my goal of supporting girls just like you, I started The Marvellous Girls Club. I realised that you cannot do better than you know. Oprah Winfrey often says that "When you know better, you do better."[6] We are all a product of the information that we have received in life. If you lack knowledge, you will not be able to attain fulfilment. Ignorance is darkness and knowledge is light. My parents could only teach me what they knew. It is not possible to give what you don't have. They didn't have the knowledge and information that is available now and so I had to learn from other sources. I am a curious girl. I learnt from books, from my older siblings, from the experiences of others and also from caring teachers who gave me words of advice in my journey into adulthood. I even learnt from music!

Hey, girl! I hope you are now able to understand why I am passionate about you – a girl! There seem to be a lot of issues around us as girls. However, I believe you are unique, and you were born for so much more than you know.

In the next chapter, I will help you understand why your teenage years are critical and the potential effects of wasting this precious time in your life. You will then better understand why I don't want you to live a life of regret.

Reflection:

Write down your experiences at school and the way you feel about school in general.

_____

_____

_____

_____

_____

_____

_____

What are some of the issues you're facing right now?

_____

_____

_____

_____

_____

_____

CHAPTER 2

THE IMPORTANCE OF YOUR TEENAGE YEARS

> *"I love being a teen because you don't have all the responsibilities of an adult yet."*
> —*Elizabeth Gillies*[7]

Many girls from my generation didn't understand how vital their teenage years were. There was no training or guidance for them in our journey to adulthood. For some of us, the focus was a good education and career, but for others, life just happened. Even though we received a good education, we were still very uneducated in terms of life experience "and didn't have a self-development guide needed to handle challenges and mistakes. For many, priorities were wrong mostly as a result of the influences of our cultures and environments. In some countries today, girls still do not have access to education. Cultural practices like early marriage are still going on in countries like Somalia. Some parents use their daughters as a source of income by trading them for a dowry – the payment made by a suitor for a wife. Some cultures still do not believe that girls *deserve* an education. Girls are prepared to stay at home doing house chores and looking after younger siblings while boys go to school. As a result of these cultural influences, many girls do not see the need to compete with boys. They feel out of place, especially in mixed-gender schools.

As a baby girl, you were not so aware of the world around you. Your only focus was on your parents and family. As you grew up, you were busy playing and running around. There were no cares or worries on your mind. You may remember crying or falling ill, but those small troubles were nothing for you to worry about because as soon as you became well, you were back to normal again. I still remember playing and running around with the boys and girls in my neighbourhood until the age of eleven. We were happy and carefree.

The first awareness that told us we were growing up was when we were leaving primary school to enter secondary school. That was the first time my friends and I felt anxious. We could no longer run around and play hide and seek like we used to. Our discussions were now about the school we wanted to attend. When the time came for us to go to secondary school, we were separated. Many of us ended up in different secondary schools. The secondary schools were more extensive – having larger buildings than primary schools, and there were many more students and teachers as well!

A new stage in our lives had begun. It will have begun for you also, if you are transitioning from primary to secondary school—you will have similar experiences. For many, this change will not be easy, but it is a change we all have to go through.

As you are facing the change that comes from changing schools, your body is also changing. While these physical changes will start late for some, for others, they will start early. Many will start the process as early as age nine. These changes can often become confusing, and it's worse still if you are trying to adjust to being in secondary school. You'll start to notice that your breasts are developing. And soon after, menstruation begins.

At this time, there are also changes going on in your brain. Your brain cells are multiplying, trying to make the vital connections to enable you to grow and develop. All of these changes are needed to help you become a well-formed adult.

The rapid changes occurring in your brain often cause your moods to swing several times during the day. You may be happy being with your friend one minute and the next you are upset to the point of crying. There are times when you may feel like crying for no explicable reason. As a teenager, this is confusing and can be worrying. You may start to think you are crazy, but you are perfectly normal. All of these experiences are part of your healthy development. I went through it too. Your actions and reactions may shock even you so you can imagine how shocked your parents will get when you scream, shout, slam the doors, get upset over little things and burst out crying!

Hey, girl! Your teenage years are so crucial because of these changes. It is the season of rapid growth. This growth may be very confusing and challenging, but it is needed nonetheless. How successful you are at navigating through these physical and psychological changes will determine how balanced and integrated you are as a young adult.

I remember getting so moody when I was a teenager and crying because I felt so miserable. I didn't understand why I was feeling that way. When my mum would ask if I was okay, I would answer in the affirmative. She would then ask me why I was crying, and I would say that I didn't know. And that was the truth. I guess crying was my way of letting out my pent-up emotions. For some of you, it may be different. However, I want you to know that you are not crazy. This is all normal, and we only wish our mums could know and understand this too.

The other exciting part of your growing up is the sense of achieving adulthood. You suddenly start feeling like you are grown-up. You don't want to be treated like a child anymore. You may even begin to wear some of your mum's or elder sister's clothes. As much as you want to feel like an adult, the truth is that you still have a lot of growing up to do. Don't be in a hurry to do adult stuff. There is a lot for you to learn first.

Hey, girl! Your teen years lead you, physically, mentally and emotionally into adulthood.

Even though you are growing up, you still do not have the responsibilities of an adult. You are still under the care of your parents or guardians. Your upkeep is still their obligation. You do not worry so much about the things that bother adults. For example, you worry about getting good grades, you worry about your changing body and whether your clothes fit, your hair, your looks and your friends. Besides this, you are not financially responsible. I must admit that some teenagers may find themselves becoming adults sooner than others as they may be accountable for taking care of themselves. This may be as a result of the absence of any parent or guardian. If you are in the kind of situation where you have to care for yourself, there are still a lot of things you can do to make the most of this season of your life.

The teen years are the stage when your mind is maturing. You are going through physical, mental and emotional changes. The whole process of how you develop and what experiences you have in your teenage years, lays the foundation for your adult life. During this time, you form an opinion about many things that will last a lifetime. It is essential that in your teenage years, you don't lose control of your ever-raging hormones. Rather, try to make choices without allowing your hormones and emotions to dictate your actions.

Everyone has to go through this critical phase of life. Our experiences may be different, but the choices we make and the way we handle our mistakes will affect us as we grow into adulthood. You don't have to grow up hating your behaviour as a teenager. You can make the most of it. You can live it and enjoy it.

In summary, your teenage years are critical because they are:

- a time of changing from a child to an adult,
- a time when your brain is making the most connections and growth,
- a time of so many confusing thoughts and emotions,
- a time when you get influenced,
- a time when you get to decide what you want to be in life,
- a time to establish your sense of self,
- a time of freedom and fewer responsibilities, and
- a time when you have the most energy and best health.

Reflection:

What are some changes you're experiencing now as a teenager or young adult?

_____

_____

_____

_____

_____

_____

_____

Do you understand these changes?

_____

_____

_____

_____

_____

_____

_____

Are you getting confused or emotional?

_____

_____

_____

_____

_____

_____

_____

_____

CHAPTER 3

THE EFFECTS OF A WASTED TEENAGE LIFE

> *"Do not watch your life melt away just like that for life is too precious to waste it doing nothing."*
> *–Sunday Adelaja*[8]

I said earlier that your time as a teenager and young adult is the most important in your journey of life. You have the opportunity to make the best use of your time and not waste these years. One common way young people spend their time these days is on social media. The need to socialise without setting boundaries is making many young people neglect the more important work they should be focused on, like reading or developing their physical and social skills. Many have become addicts to social media. Social media should not become a stumbling block on your road to success. [9]

Other are wasting their teen years with television, movies, video games and entertainment. Some idle time away hanging out with friends at odd places. I believe it's crucial to have some time for fun in your life. However, it's counter-productive to spend too much time pursuing activities which do not result in improvement for the world or your own life.

Some girls' teen years are halted by early pregnancies. Having kids at such a young age and without preparation has left many young girls miserable, unhappy, stressed, and incapable of taking care of themselves let alone their children.

Remember, we said that your teenage years are critical because you are growing up and your mind is maturing. You are laying the foundation of your life at this time. As a teenager, you generally have the most energy and the best health. You are also at a phase when you have the most free time that you are ever likely to have. If you do not make the best use of this phase of your life, that could become a disadvantage to you in your adult life.

Here are some things that may affect you as an adult if you waste your teenage years:

1. You will be confused and lack focus. Confusion and a lack of focus are seen in many women today as a result of not making the most of their teenage years. They are not clear about what they want to be or achieve in life, so they keep jumping from one thing to another. They have no future career or life goals and hence, they have no focus.

2. You may develop some harmful or destructive habits. Many hurtful and damaging patterns some women display as adults started from when they were teenagers. Some got into the habit of smoking, drinking and partying all through their teen years. They thought they would be able to stop when they wanted to, but the habit became a force stronger than them.

3. You may have low self-esteem and lack confidence. When you do not invest your time as a teenager in educating and empowering yourself, you then lack confidence and have low self-esteem. Your teen years are the time for self-development and growth.

4. You may become a woman who is not able to stand by her values. Also, if you have not learnt to know yourself and the things that you believe in, you could easily be swayed into doing things you do not want to do. If you don't want to become a woman who can be easily influenced, then you need to develop your own values.

5. You may suffer abuse in your relationships and not even recognise it. A lack of confidence and low self-esteem will ultimately lead to damage and violence in any relationship. When you do not have a clear understanding of what a healthy relationship is, abuse is almost inevitable.

6. You may live a life without purpose. Wasting your teenage years also means you will lack the awareness that you are here for a reason. If you don't know this, you will live life without

a clear goal and vision. This is the reason many are confused and depressed.

7. You may be successful in your career and yet have no fulfilment or actual happiness. It is not enough to have a good job. Ultimately, being fulfilled and happy is more important. When you spend your teenage years not knowing the difference between having a successful career and being happy, you will have a good career but take a while to realise that life is much more than that. For some, this realisation may come too late.

8. You may not be resilient and may crumble easily under the challenges of life. Many women did not develop their resilience when they were young. As a result, they end up smoking and drinking alcohol to cope with life's challenges. Many end up in mental institutions as a result of emotional breakdowns. Building resilience is vital to help protect you from developing depression and other mental health problems.

9. You may not be able to keep a job. If you have not developed discipline, the right attitude and excellent social skills as a teenager, you might end up becoming a misfit and an antisocial person in the workplace. Your teenage years are the time to begin developing discipline and social skills. If you don't, you may find yourself changing jobs for no convincing reason.

10. . You may not be able to maintain healthy relationships. Your social skills will be weak if you do not develop emotional intelligence and exceptional social skills as a teen.

11. You may become needy. If you have not prepared yourself to be self-sufficient, you may live your life depending on others to meet your needs. Being needy is worse if you find yourself as a young mother. It will make you a burden and pain to others and cause them to avoid you. People may take advantage of you, and this may also lead to abuse.

12. You may become self-absorbed. A self-absorbed person is not pleasant to be around. The world does not revolve around you or anyone else. When you live your life thinking that everything is about you, you will end up with rejections and isolation. Many women who have wasted their teenage years

living only for themselves or engrossed in social media become self-absorbed and social misfits in their families, workplaces and society at large as adults.

Hey, girl! I believe that as you journey into adulthood, you won't like to look back and realise you wasted your teenage years. You can now see why it is essential to make the most of your adolescence. You need to start laying the foundation and begin developing yourself and the right attributes you want to embody as you grow into an adult. You can make this the most productive time of your life. You can live a life of happiness and fulfilment.

In this book, you will find the self-development tools you need to make the most of your years as a teenager and young adult. Don't let this phase of your life be all about boys. If you do, you will end up with pain and regret. Take the ideas shared in this book and begin to develop yourself and dream about the life you want for yourself. There is so much for you to start doing now as a young person. Don't limit yourself; instead, explore and expose yourself to information and the knowledge you need to reach your full potential.

> *"Being happy is something that each of us determines;*
> *it is not something that we find outside of ourself; it is*
> *within us and our choice."*
> *– Catherine Pulsifer*[10]

You can determine your happiness and create the life you want now, as a teenager.

I believe you can now better understand why your teenage years are critical and why you should not waste this most productive time of your life. This time of your life isn't supposed to be boring; it's supposed to be exciting!

In the next chapter, to help you better understand the importance of developing yourself in the teenage years, I will be discussing the subject of Identity and why you must know who you are.

Reflection:

What are some things that you're doing now that you need to change?

_____

_____

_____

_____

_____

_____

_____

_____

Do you think about the type of person you want to become?

_____

_____

_____

_____

_____

_____

_____

From the list above about the possible dangers of wasting your teenage years, which are the dangers that you would like to protect yourself against most?

_____

_____

_____

_____

_____

_____

_____

_____

CHAPTER 4

IDENTITY CRISIS

> *"The easiest thing to be in the world is you. The most difficult thing to be is what other people want you to be. Don't let them put you in that position."*
> *– Leo Buscaglia[11]*

According to Webster's New World College Dictionary, an identity crisis is "the condition of being uncertain of one's feelings about oneself, especially with regards to character, goals, and origins, occurring especially in adolescence as a result of growing up under disruptive, fast-changing conditions."

Growing up as a young girl in Nigeria, I remember running free around the neighbourhood and playing with everyone—boys and girls. We didn't have a care in the world.

Things started to get a bit different when it was time to sit the primary school graduating exams. The anxiety around going to secondary started setting in. Many of us did get into the school of our choice and while some of us found ourselves in a different school than our friends, others ended up in the same school.

I found myself attending an all-girls school. I also noticed that we- boys and girls, were no longer free to run around and play together the way we used to. We were suddenly becoming self-conscious. For some, our bodies were changing already too. It was a very confusing and lonely time. I wasn't prepared for these changes at all. My mother didn't tell me anything. I missed my friends and our playtimes. I had more responsibilities with regards to helping at home and a new level of freedom too. I was in charge of doing the dishes and keeping the living room tidy. I was also allowed to hang out with my friends as long as I had done my chores. I was no longer a child. I needed to take care of myself more. I was changing physically and no longer needed my mum to tell me when to take a bath or change my clothes or do my hair. I needed to know myself better as I took charge of my life.

While I was in school as a teenager, I started noticing changes in the other girls. For some strange reason, I didn't like what I saw. I told myself that if this was how girls behaved, then I did not want to be one of them. Of course, I was in a girls' school. I was a class monitor, as we called it back then, but I was not impressed with girls. I was not comfortable with being one. I had my close friends back then, but I related more to the boys around me who were attending an all-boys school.

What was it about girls that I didn't like?

- Girls were too noisy and chatty.
- Girls were too emotional and were always having arguments over little things.
- Girls were always seeking attention from boys.
- Girls didn't talk about intelligent things.
- Girls were weaker than boys.
- Girls were not as smart as boys.
- Girls were too conscious about their looks.
- Girls got hurt and angry quickly.

Hey, girl! can you relate to this?

All of these complaints were misconceptions that I had probably developed because of the culture and society in which I was growing up. A society where females were considered to be inferior to males. A community that did not pay any attention to girls or consider them as being important. Even though some cultures are changing, many still do not treat the girl–child with respect. My understanding of what made a girl is was very skewed.

My Identity Crisis

Noticing these negative behaviours and attitudes towards the girl–child, I decided that no one was better than me, and therefore, I would rather hang out with boys so as not to be seen as inferior to them. I had an Identity crisis. I felt I should have been a boy. I wanted to be stronger and not be considered weak. I wanted to be as intelligent as any boy around me, if not smarter. I hated that I got emotional and cried sometimes. Of course, I was growing up, and my brain was rapidly growing too. Before long, my breasts started developing, and I also began to go through menstruation. I had mood swings. I was confused about what was happening to me. My body was going through changes I wasn't prepared to acknowledge And I was becoming more self-conscious. I didn't like any of it. Where was that girl who used to run around playing in the neighbourhood? That girl was growing up.

It didn't take long for me to understand that I was a girl, and no matter how much I hung out with boys, they would always see me as a girl. And they would treat me like a girl.

So, what was I supposed to do? I needed to accept myself as a girl and become the best version of me. I realised that being a girl did not make me inferior to anyone. Being a girl did not make me weaker or less intelligent than a boy. A girl today is much different from who a girl was considered to be in my days growing up. We now talk of gender equality, of the fact that no one is better than you. Yes, we are all equally gifted and blessed. We only have to discover what makes us unique. I am a girl—I am proud to be a girl because I now know who I am.

The important thing here is to know who you are. To know yourself and to live in the awareness of who you are.

How do you define yourself as a girl?

What does being a girl mean to you?

Who are You?

Did you say your name? Well, you are not just your name.

Did you say the name of your school and your class? That does not say who you are!

Okay, maybe you want to tell me about your background too? But that is not who *you* are.

Oh, your family! Should I have known that? Do you have a great family name? Is your dad a public figure? That is not who you are!

You are not the family in which you were born. You are not the clothes you wear or the school you attend. You are not the experiences you may be having right now, whether negative or positive. None of these define you. You are more than all of these!

Hey, girl! Your ability to know this will give you a strong sense of identity. Having accurate knowledge of who you are is essential if you do not want to go through an identity crisis. The situation you're in right now doesn't matter.

> *"You can never meet your potential until you truly learn to love yourself."*
> — *Teresa Collins*[12]

I agree with Teresa Collins; your ability to fulfil your potential begins with your identity. Knowing who you are and accepting yourself for that is very important as you grow into an adult.

Born for a Purpose

True identity must first be rooted in the Sovereign being—God, who is the creator of everything. He created the whole of humanity, and He blessed all of His creation. Irrespective of your gender, everyone is made in His Image.

Hey, girl! You are uniquely designed and blessed. You are gifted and equipped with everything you need to succeed on earth. You only need to pay attention, and you will discover your unique attributes.

There is a reason why we are not all the same. Every one of us is packaged for a specific assignment to fulfil on earth. You were born for a purpose. You were not a mistake. You were born as a solution to resolve an issue in the world. Some will discover this early, as was the case with Malala Yousafzi (Born July 12, 1997).

She is the girl who is known to fight for the girl–child's right to education. As a girl growing up in Pakistan, the Taliban were threatening to close down schools for girls. She defied the Taliban and demanded that girls be allowed to receive an education. Malala became widely known after she was shot in the head by the Taliban in Pakistan. Malala survived following surgery in the United Kingdom. Today she is an advocate for girl's education and is the youngest person to win a Nobel Peace prize. Malala found her purpose early and she is living it. [13]

Hey, girl! Who you are is more than your name, how you look and the clothes you put on. There is so much more that you are created to accomplish. The question of identity is the root cause of the issues that many teenagers and young adults face.

How can you Know Yourself?

To know who you are, you need to answer the following questions:

- What are the things that interest you?
- What are the things that you love doing?
- What are the things that make you happy or sad?
- What can you spend all your time doing without getting tired?
- What are you naturally good at doing?

When you can identify these things, they become part of your understanding of yourself and help you learn your purpose–why you are here.

Other Misconception about Teenage Girls

I have mentioned my own misconceptions about being a girl. However, I also realise that there are misconceptions that others, including parents, will have about you as a teenage girl.

Here are a few of the most common misconceptions held by adults about teenage girls:[14]

Girls are still young and have no experience.

They think you are too young and lack the life experience to know anything about serious matters. The truth is that many teenage girls have had plenty of difficult things happen to them in their short lives. I remember when we lost one of our classmates to sickle cell anaemia in secondary school. Another friend was having a difficult time with her mother at home as she was an only child. Her mother was over-protective of her and this was very frustrating. Another girl was also dealing with the divorce of her parents. And another lost her dad just a year before we graduated from secondary school. A lot of girls just like you are facing some hard challenges already, and this becomes part of their life experiences and also results in them gaining maturity.

Girls nowadays are lazy and disrespectful.

Some adults will think you are all lazy and rude, and don't give a damn about education. However, we know this is not true. Many teen girls do care, and work to gain the skills they need to succeed. Many girls will love and respect people they admire. I am sure you have people around you too that you admire and respect.

You are not depressed, you want attention.

Some adults think you'll say you are depressed so that you can get attention. As teens, it is reasonable to feel down sometimes, and you don't feel this way to get attention. The hormonal changes in your body, coupled with rapid brain development, may often cause your moods to change. Occasionally you may experience real depression and will need to talk to someone to get help.

Girls are easy to understand.

They will think they understand you even when they don't. It's normal to get frustrated with parents and the adults around you because they don't understand you. You sometimes want to express yourselves to them so they can understand how you're feeling. Unfortunately, many adults are so busy that they do not have the time to listen.

Girls are spoilt.

They think you are spoilt when it comes to food, clothing and gadgets. They think you are only looking for enjoyment. Your growing body needs food, so you always need to eat. And your body is growing, so you still want new clothes. Also, gadgets like a laptop or even an e-reader are necessary for school and are required these days. Having these things doesn't mean you are spoilt.

Girls nowadays are not serious.

They think you are blasé and not as hardworking as they are. Many girls are so diligent that they have even started businesses as teenagers. It is not uncommon to find young entrepreneurs nowadays.

Girls have it easy nowadays.

The most significant misconception is that school life is always enjoyable and fun. Well, that is not always so. They don't know that you have to deal with problems like poor relationships with family, friends and boyfriends or girlfriends. Other issues that you deal with are low self-esteem, stress from the exam-oriented educational system, and high hopes and expectations from parents and teachers. In short, your life as a teenager is not an easy one.

Girls nowadays are so laid back.

They think, that you have no drive or motivation to do things. Many girls do take up leading roles in sports and at school. They are known to excel in the areas they're gifted in.

Girls nowadays are not preparing for the future.

They tend to believe you lack the initiative to prepare yourself for the future. In most cases, this isn't true. You *can* go that extra mile to achieve things when you are determined to. Of course, as a teenager, you like to enjoy your free time by going out or pursuing personal interests. That does not mean you aren't serious about your studies and your future. You can enjoy yourself and also make sure you work hard as well.

These are just a few misconceptions that adults—even your parents—may have about you as a teenager. Do you agree or disagree with them? Throughout this book, I will be sharing tips on how to behave so that the adults in your life do not hold these misconceptions about you.

Reflection:

How do you define yourself?

_____

_____

_____

_____

_____

_____

_____

Have you experienced an Identity crisis?

_____

_____

_____

_____

_____

_____

_____

What are the things about girls that you don't like?

_____

_____

_____

_____

_____

_____

_____

What are the things you've noticed about yourself that make you who you are?

_____

_____

_____

_____

_____

_____

_____

CHAPTER 5

WHAT TYPE OF GIRL DO YOU WANT TO BECOME?

"To find yourself, think for yourself." – Socrates[15]

I have taken you through some of the misconceptions that adults have about girls. Many people think you are lazy, disrespectful, and that you lack the initiative to prepare yourself for the future. The question born out of these misconceptions is: What kind of girl do you want to be?

Do you want to be known as an irresponsible girl who cannot be relied upon to do anything for herself or to help anyone else?

Hey, girl! To start thinking about this now is very important. Whatever you decide will inform who you'll be and how far you'll go in life.

You can decide what type of girl you want to become. You have that power in your hands. You can look at yourself in the mirror right now and tell yourself who you want to see and that is:

- a compassionate girl,
- a loving and considerate girl,
- an ambitious and successful girl,
- an intelligent girl,
- a kind and generous girl.
- a trustworthy girl.
- a moral and principled girl,
- a godly and dedicated girl, or
- a modest girl.

Hey, girl! If you want to make the most of your teenage years, you can choose to be any of the above. Or, you can choose to be lazy, unambitious and irresponsible.

It doesn't matter how academically brilliant you are or how significant your background is: you must decide what type of girl you want to become. Remember, I mentioned earlier that you are not your name or the clothes you wear or your family background. These do not define you. You are who you decide to be!

> *"I can be a better me than anyone can." – **Diana Ross**[16]*

Diana Ross is an American singer who sold over 100 million albums. And yes, I agree with her: you *can* be a better you! As Socrates said, you have to think for yourself. No one can do that for you. YOU must decide.

An example of a girl who is defining her own identity is Greta Thunberg, the Swedish 17-year old who is cutting class to fight climate change. Greta has become very popular in the news of late as a result of her activism. She described herself in a report as being a "painfully introverted, slightly built nobody, waking at 6 am to prepare for school and to head back home at 3 pm." She went on to say, "nothing was happening in my life. I have always been that girl in the back who doesn't say anything." Greta didn't think she could make a difference but today she has visited many countries and campaigned for world leaders to do more about the Climate. She has become an internationally recognised climate activist.[17]

You can also begin defining your own identity right now. I don't think you are too young to take responsibility for your own life. Many young teenagers like you have taken responsibility for themselves and have become people to reckon with in society.

I mentioned Malala Yousafzai in the previous chapter—here are some quotes from her about defining yourself:

"I used to think I had to wait to be an adult to lead. But I have learnt that even a child's voice can be heard around the world."

She also went on to say this:

"Often, we think we are too young, or our ideas may not work, and we need to grow up to bring change. I say no. Whatever you want to do now, you can do it now."[18]

Malala is so right. You may think you are too small or too young. I used to feel the same as a teenager, but I realise then that many young people like me are taking responsibility for their lives. They are not waiting for others to decide for them. You get to decide what kind of girl you want to be right now.

Hey, girl! Think for yourself.

You can see now that having a sense of Identity is very important if you are to maximise your life as a teenager. If Malala had died from the gunshot to her head, she would still have lived a meaningful life because she would have been making a change. She invested her life in fighting for what she believed in. Even though she was just a young girl, she knew who she was and she fought for her right to get an education. Greta is also fighting for what she believes in, which is a better, healthier world. What do you want to be known for? In the next chapter, we shall be looking at the role our dreams play in helping us define our identity.

Reflection:

Who are you?

_____

_____

_____

_____

_____

_____

_____

How do you want to be remembered?

_____

_____

_____

_____

_____

_____

_____

Do you think you can be more responsible?

_____

_____

_____

_____

_____

_____

_____

_____

Do you think you're too young to make a difference?

_____

_____

_____

_____

_____

_____

_____

How can you make a difference right now, where you are?

_____

_____

_____

_____

_____

_____

_____

CHAPTER 6

A GIRL AND HER DREAMS

> *"The future belongs to those who believe in the beauty*
> *of their dreams." – Eleanor Roosevelt*[19]

You can see now that it is vital to know who you are. Your Identity gives you the confidence to make a difference in your world. You don't have to be like anybody but yourself. Just improve yourself and stand up for what you believe in!

Having a strong sense of identity also has an impact on your dreams. As young children, one of the popular questions you would have been faced with is: "What do you want to be when you grow up?" From an early age, everyone has a dream of what they want to be when they grow up. The ability to dream is a gift given to every human on earth. We were all born with a dream. Every creature on this earth is here as a solution to resolve an issue. Everything is here for a purpose. The sun and moon are here to give light and the clouds to give rain. We wear clothes to protect us from cold or heat, and shoes to protect our feet. Everything made was for a specific purpose and each of these purposes began as a dream in someone's heart.

One story about dreams that inspires me a lot is that of a woman known as Tererai Trent. She is a Zimbabwean-America woman who grew up in the village of Zvipani in Zimbabwe. She was not allowed to go to school, in part as a result of poverty but mostly because she was a girl. Boys were the only ones allowed in school because they were seen as the breadwinners of tomorrow while girls were only prepared for marriage. Tererai had to teach herself to read and write from her brother's books and eventually, she started doing her brother's homework. When the teacher discovered this, he pleaded with her father to allow her to attend classes. However, it didn't take long before her father withdrew her from school and gave her away for marriage in exchange for a cow! Can you believe that?

Tererai was a mother of four children before she was eighteen, and without a high school diploma. However, she still nursed her dream for education in her heart. Her husband beat her for wanting an education. In 1991, an American woman named Jo Luck, from Heifer International, visited her village and asked every woman about their greatest dream. Tererai didn't think her goals were achievable after being married and having children, but she spoke them out anyway. She said she wanted to go to America and get a bachelor's degree, a master's, and then a PhD. The visit by the woman from America inspired her to pursue her dreams. When she left the meeting, her mother encouraged her to write down her dreams. She wrote them down, put the paper in a scrap of tin, and buried it. [20]

These were her dreams. It looked impossible for her to achieve them because of her culture and background. But even though she was married at such a young age, she pursued her dreams. Although she was poor, she believed in her dreams. She worked hard to get an education. For eight years she struggled to write her exams and got admitted into a University in the United States of America. While in America, amidst so much poverty and struggles with her children, she got not only a bachelor's degree, but a master's degree and also a PhD. She never gave up on herself. Today she is recognised as one of the ten most inspiring women in the world.

Why is it Vital for you to Have a Dream?

From Tererai's story, you can see that if she hadn't had a dream, she would not have fulfilled her potential. While being a wife and mother is good, Tererai wanted to fulfil her own dreams. No one would have been talking about her today if she had accepted her fate in the village. Her parents didn't have a dream for her except for her to be married. For many of us, our parents' dream may be for us to get good grades, go to college and get a good job. Many parents even go to the extent of choosing a career path for their children. It could be a career they dreamt of for themselves but were not able to pursue, so they want their children to follow that path. Maybe it is to be a doctor, a lawyer, an accountant or an engineer. While it may be easy for some to pursue the route set for them by their parents, for others, this may be the beginning of an unhappy life. Even though Trent's parents wanted her married off, she had a different dream for herself. It does not matter what goals your parents have for you; you also need to have a goal for yourself. Your destiny is in your own hands. Trent did what her parents wanted, but it didn't stop her from pursuing her dreams. You can create the life you want to live and it starts now. Like Trent, write down the future you want and be bold enough to pursue it. Do not let anyone make you do what you do not want to do. Remember, we have said that you were born unique. You may look exactly like your mum, but you are not her or even your dad! You are different from them and everyone else. Be you and do you. Listen to yourself and the things you desire to do and to be.

> *"Don't let the noise of others' opinions drown out your inner voice. And most important, dare to follow your heart and intuition."*- **Steve Jobs**[21]

Hey, girl! What are your dreams? You can begin to dream out loud now! Maybe your goal in life is to be an advocate for girls' empowerment or to become a World Champion in a particular sport or activity. Or you could become a researcher, who will change the world with a discovery. You could even be a great politician.

Can your dreams come true? Yes, they can. Many people have had their dreams come true. You would think that Trent would not have been able to achieve her goal after being married off at the age of eleven and having four children before she was eighteen! But she did accomplish her intentions to get a bachelor's, masters and a PhD! Was it easy for her? No! Making your dream come true is never going to be easy. There will be challenges and obstacles, but your dreams are still achievable. Here are some steps to follow to achieve your dreams:

1. Ask yourself: What do I want to do right now, so that in a year, I won't have regrets? You can only regret the chances you didn't take.

2. Ask yourself: What are my hopes, dreams, goals and aspirations? Never let anyone tell you that your ideas are silly or unimportant.

3. Know your worth as an Individual. Don't let anyone make you think less of yourself. No one is better than you. You are unique and Marvellous!

4. Ask yourself; what is my risk tolerance and what are my your strengths?

5. Tell others about your dreams and what you want to achieve.

6. If something speaks to your heart, don't hold back—JUMP! Step out in a leap of faith. Believe in yourself.

7. Make progress, not perfection. Striving for perfection is the quickest way to sabotage your journey to achieving your dreams. What happens is that you don't do it correctly the first time, and you give up, thinking that you can't do it at all. Keep making steady progress toward your goal (even if it is slow going!), and before you know it, you will be there.

8. Identify what your passions are. What excites you so much that you can't wait to jump out of bed in the morning to get started? Pursue that with a passion.

9. Making your dreams happen is about using your fears and frustrations as fuel for transformation. Living successfully requires risk and courage. I know this first-hand. Don't be afraid to fail. If Plan A doesn't work out, go to Plan B…and then Plan C. You will find a way to make your dreams come true.

10. Take time for yourself every day. Even if you can spare just 30 minutes from your busy schedule, do something that's soul-

satisfying. Spend time meditating and visualising yourself in the middle of living your dream life.[22]

Visualisation involves picturing in your mind the outcome of something before it's happened. One significant benefit of visualisation is a boost in confidence. Imagining yourself achieving the goals you want to achieve makes them more tangible—and in turn, you start believing in your ability to get there.[23]

As crucial as dreams are, many are not able to achieve them. There will always be circumstances in life that may get in the way of us achieving our dreams. For many of us, we didn't even know the importance of having a personal goal when we were growing up. We were going through life and living by chance, hoping that everything will work out just fine. However, life is not to be left to chance. Life is predictable. Yes, things may happen that may be out of your control, but you can still be in charge of your life. There are things you can begin to do to achieve the future in your dreams. You can create your destiny.

Here are some reasons why you need to chase after your dreams and not give up:

1. The secret of living is giving. If you follow your dreams, you'll have things worth sharing with others: hope, inspiration, and purpose.

2. Dreams inspire us to be hopeful and young-at-heart.

3. Great dreamers are independent. They understand the power that they hold within them to make a difference in the world.

4. Dreams fill you with a positive perspective. Negative drama is obsolete when you are passionate about following your dreams.

5. When you pursue your goals, you come to understand failure leads you from where you are to where you want to go.

6. Dreamers understand that age is irrelevant.

7. Dreamers face fear with courage because they see challenges as opportunities to feel invigorated and alive.[24]

When you accomplish your dream, you are the first to see and experience it as it unfolds. You can share your accomplishments with the rest of the world and enjoy the magic as you reach your goal. Tererai Trent is an inspiration today because she dared to pursue her dreams.

> *"All our dreams can come true if we have the courage to pursue them."*
> *— Walt Disney* [25]

When Life Gets in the Way

Don't give up on your dreams just because life gets in the way. It could be that you suddenly find yourself pregnant or married early and have to drop out of college. Maybe your financial circumstances make it look impossible to pursue your dreams. Or it could even be that you find yourself without your parents and have to be in foster care. No matter what the circumstances are, your dreams are achievable if you will only dare to pursue them.

Here are some examples of women who were still able to pursue their dreams even though life tried to get in the way:

We all hear about Oprah Winfrey today, but how many of us know her background? Oprah grew up in poverty and was sexually abused as a child. When she found out she was pregnant, she ran away from home. Oprah had her baby at fourteen, but the baby died soon after birth. She didn't allow this incident to define her. Despite many obstacles, she pursued her dreams to become the highest-ranking TV show host in America. Today Oprah is the CEO of her television network, OWN TV. [26]

Another woman worth mentioning is J.K. Rowling, the author of the *Harry Potter* series. Rowling found herself in poverty and homeless after a failed marriage. She also had a daughter to care for, and all she had left was her dreams. She didn't allow her failure to break her; instead, she was able to discover who she was—with hope, a big idea, and a typewriter. Today J.K. Rowling is ranks among the most inspiring women in the world. Here is what she's said about the experience:

> *""Failure gave me an inner security that I had never attained by passing examinations. Failure taught me things about myself that I could have learned no other way."* [27]

Sometimes we may *fail in life*, but we must know that *failure is learning*. We must not allow our omissions or mistakes to become limitations or obstacles in the pursuit of our dreams and purposes.

I love the story of Montana Brown. She is a woman who had to fight for her life against cancer twice during her childhood, and she survived. Her experiences and contact with kind paediatric nurses during her stays in the hospital made her dream of becoming a nurse. At 24, Montana achieved that goal. On her first day at work at the Children's Healthcare of Atlanta non-profit, she wrote in a Facebook post:

> *"Never in a million years did I think that at the age of 24 I would have achieved my biggest and wildest dream—to work at the hospital where I was treated as a child/teenager. It's amazing and crazy and awesome, and I'm SO excited to work with such an inspirational organisation!!"*[28]

Hey, girl! It doesn't matter what happens or gets in the way as you journey into adulthood; you can turn it around. You can achieve a dream that helps others and gives back some of the love and care you received when you needed it most. The story of Montana teaches us this lesson.

Have the courage to follow your heart. Your heart will never steer you in the wrong direction. It is through your heart that the universe speaks to you, and I guarantee that you WILL find your dream in that place where your mind meets your heart and your soul.

Hey, girl! What is your greatest dream? If you don't have a goal, then I want to invite you to start dreaming—and start dreaming

BIG. Your dreams are valid, and they are achievable. Have a picture of the future you desire. Your goal may not necessarily be about you but about the change you want to bring to the world. A real dream will give you respect, wealth (material and non-material) and most importantly, a reason for living. Start believing in your vision and your dreams will come true.

One of my goals was to write a book. I read a lot of books while growing up, and I still do. I remember writing a play script for a drama presentation in secondary school. But most of all, I wanted to write books to share my experiences with the world. That you are reading this book is proof that dreams come true.

I believe you can now understand how important it is for you to have a dream. It is important also for you to know that dreams do come true. So never give up on your goals. In the next chapter, we shall be looking at the importance of time, and why you must value it. Time is life.

Reflection:

What are your dreams?

_____

_____

_____

_____

_____

_____

_____

Do you believe that dreams can come true?

_____

_____

_____

_____

_____

_____

_____

If you don't have a dream, you need to start dreaming now. Write down some of your your goals.

_____

_____

_____

_____

_____

_____

_____

Why's it essential to pursue your dreams?

_____

_____

_____

_____

_____

_____

_____

CHAPTER 7

TIME IS LIFE – DON'T WASTE IT

> *"Time is free, but it's priceless. You can't own it, but you can use it. You can't keep it, but you can spend it. Once you've lost it, you can never get it back." —Harvey Mackay*[29]

The most significant wealth we all have here as humans is the wealth of time. The way you value time and how you manage it will improve your life. Your future is created by what you do today, not tomorrow.

> *"Time is more valuable than money. You can get more money, but you cannot get more time." —Jim Rohn*[30]

Here is an experiment for you to do. Get a group of your friends together. Set a timer to go off in thirty seconds. Ask your friends to close their eyes and only open them after 30 seconds. You will discover that some will open their eyes earlier while others will open their eyes later. Everyone has their own perception of what time is. Even though we all have the same 24 hours in a day—or 30 seconds, in the exercise—we experience and use this time in different ways. Some of us experience time as a short period, and others experience it as long.

There are usually three things we can do with our time. We can waste time, spend time and invest time. You get to decide which one to do at every point in your life.

Wasting Time

To waste time is to be engaged in activities that yield no meaningful results for you. You might decide to watch a program on TV or chat on your phone (this is not bad but mindless TV and mindless chatting is) when you could be making better use of your time by studying or reading a book.

Spending Time

When you spend time, you get a reward for it. Reading a book or studying a subject that interests you will increase your knowledge significantly compared to spending time just chatting with a friend. We get paid for the work that we do as adults, and we spend time mostly by engaging in this type of work. As a teenager or young adult in education, the reward for spending your time at school is getting good grades. It could be that you are into sports or music or any other extracurricular activity. Your reward for pursuing these will be receiving a gold medal or winning a competition, all because you spent hours practising and becoming exceptional in that area.

Investing Time

Investing time means multiplying your life by engaging in activities that will bear fruits- you will have tangible results at the end of it.. To convert time into a product is to increase your life. You can invest your time in writing a book, coming up with an idea for a product or releasing a new song. By doing so, you leave a legacy. Investing time is the best way to use time as it pays off even when you are dead. You can invest your time right now in productive activities, even apart from just going to school. You will be surprised at how many different things you can do even now if you invest your time wisely.[31]

I did mention in the previous chapter that the teenage years are times of fewer responsibilities. As a result, many teenagers do not seem to realise just how fast time flies. You are not going to be in school forever; neither are you going to be a teenager all your life. If you have a time-piece around you now, you will notice that the time is ticking, tick-tock. Time waits for no one. Many of us don't seem to remember this. You will not be young all your life. You will not be strong and healthy all your life. Your parents will not be responsible for you all your life. With time, change happens. You are not too young now to have a goal for your life. Growing up, many of us didn't realise this; we lost a lot of time doing things we shouldn't have been doing, not understanding that with every passing moment, time was slipping away. Now, as adults, we suddenly want to do the things we should have done as teenagers.

Consider this story:

Jemima was carried away by the illusion of being young and free. She knew her education was important, but there were girls in school who appeared to be having more fun than she was. Even though Jemima was intelligent, being a part of a clique was attractive to her. She heard the other girls talking about all the fun things they did after school. When she became friends with these girls, they wondered why she spent so much of her time studying. They invited her to join them to attend a party. But her mum didn't give her permission to go. She was angry at her mum.

"You're a kill-joy who never allows me to have any fun," she huffed. Her mum explained that it was not okay for her to be attending parties when she should be preparing for her forthcoming exams. But Jemima wanted so much to go to the party with her friends, and so she went without her parents' knowledge. At the party, Jemima's friends were happy to see her. They welcomed her and introduced her to their boyfriends and other friends at the party. Thus, began Jemima's party lifestyle. Even though she was just 15, she would go with her friends to parties. Soon after this, she started taking 'legal highs'. She became so distracted by her friends and a new boyfriend that she began skipping school. The school alerted her parents to the changes, but when confronted, Jemima always got defensive. When the time came for her final exams, she was unprepared, of course. Jemima had panic attacks and suffered from severe anxiety. She became depressed when she didn't pass her exams. She knew she could have done so much better. She knew she was intelligent. She had just wasted her time instead of investing it in studying. Now she had to spend more time trying to make up for her grades so that she could further her education. Wouldn't it have been better if Jemima had studied more and did less partying?

Hey, girl! I wrote this story to help you understand that time does not wait for anyone. Make the most of the time you have now. If you don't, you will need to spend even more time doing something you could have done earlier if only you had paid attention.

What can you do now to maximise your teenage years and not waste them? We cannot answer this question without emphasising the importance of time.

From the day you were born, you became a product of time. Time is measured in seconds, minutes, days, months and years. So you see, time is Life! Whatever age you are now is the amount of time you have spent here on earth. To gain the benefits of time, you must do the following things.

Value Time

To maximise your time, you must make sure you convert every second and minute into value. Learn how to value time. Time is non-refundable; use it with intention. A lot of people today have no value for time; don't be among them. Value your time! You are growing, and with growth comes change. Even though you are young and energetic today, it will not always be so. There are things you can do easily now that you will not be able to do in the next ten years. This is why you should make good use of your time now.

Be Self-Aware

You must always be self-aware and ask yourself, – "What am I doing now? Am I adding value to myself or others? Why am I here?" I find myself still doing this as an adult. Do not go to bed without asking yourself the question "What have I achieved today?" You can start practising this habit now. I hate to be idle. And you should too. Make your time count. Be conscious of every passing minute and examine yourself and your activities. Your daily activities also have a lot to do with what you will achieve in the future.

Be Disciplined

Be disciplined! It takes discipline for you to make the most of your time. You may be reading a book, and then you suddenly feel like you would rather watch TV. You need the discipline to know that reading that book is of more benefit to you than watching the television show. Stay on task and finish it. Discipline is an important value to have if you are to succeed in life. We will talk about this in more detail later on.

Avoid Distractions

You must avoid distractions. We are living in an age of so many distractions. A major one is that of our mobile phones and social media. Our friends also can be a distraction. If you want to make the most of your youth, you need to be able to identify the interferences around you and avoid them. I know your friends are essential to you, but you have to be wise. As a teenager, one way I avoided distractions from my friends was to go to bed early and wake up when everyone was still sleeping so I could read in peace. Right now, social media is a significant distraction. Maybe you can have your parents keep your phone while you study and also at night when you go to bed. Don't let yourself be distracted.

Be Intentional and Purposeful

Do not be the girl who does things solely for the fun of it. You will be wasting your life if you cannot find a purpose behind every action. Always ask yourself "Why?" Why should I visit that friend? Why should I study now? Why should I join that club? Will it benefit me? Will it do me any good to attend a party when I could be studying and learning something new? How will I feel if I do not succeed at school? Don't allow the pressure from friends to make you do things you don't want to do. Do everything with intention and with a purpose in mind. You have a brain for a reason; think before you act! Question everything!

Measure your Results

Measure your life by the results you produce daily. Yes, you *can* do this. As a teenager, I had a personal timetable, besides my school timetable. You should always ask yourself "What have I done today?" Do this both at school and at home. A timetable will help you measure your daily activities. You can then see what you should accomplish daily. Remember to include some free time in your timetable. Then you can be flexible with your timetable and not feel bad if you are not able to do something you wanted to on a particular day. To test whether your timetable is working, you should be able to look at it and see what you have accomplished. It may be things like practising on the keyboard or practising your sport or even just finishing a book or an assignment.

> *"Time is a currency you can only spend once, so be careful how you spend it" - **Harmon Okinyo**[32]*

You can become great through careful use of the currency of time. Time is indeed a currency with which you can make purchases. For example, your being in school now is a transaction of time. You are using your time to obtain an education. Let's say you are learning how to play the piano or violin; after several years, you become good at it. You have just purchased that skill with Time. Time is money. Whatever you want to be or have in Life, you can buy it, if you devote enough time to it.

Here are some renowned sports celebrities who paid with time to become great in their chosen field:

It's written that Serena Williams, a professional American tennis player, spent two hours every single day practising with her father, from the age of three. Today she has won 23 Grand Slam singles titles and several Olympic gold medals. [33]

She has given so much time to playing tennis that she has become world-renowned.

Simone Biles, who is a world-class gymnast, recently made history for holding the title of the most decorated American gymnast. How did she achieve this? Biles worked for it. She used the currency of time to purchase her greatness. She's won 25 World Championship medals and 5 additional Olympic medals. Biles said this about her achievements:

> *"I think it inspires a lot of the little girls out there to go in the gym and train harder".*[34]

Name any person who has accomplished anything today, even the most brilliant person at your school, and know that they have all won these accomplishments by trading their time for them.

Hey, girl! What's the amount and quality of time you're putting into your goals? The amount of time you are willing to devote to your goals will determine what will become of your life. How much time are you putting into your practice right now? How much time are you putting into reading books? How much time are you spending on assignments? The amount and quality of time you put to your goals will determine if you are wasting your life or maximising it. Be wise in spending your time.

I hope you now understand how important time is and why you must learn to value it. The value you have for time will also determine how much you value your life. Everything you will do and become will eventually come with time. None of us knows how much time we have on this earth. While some will live longer, others' lives may be short. It's essential to make the most of our time here irrespective of how long we live. In the next chapter, I will be looking at our companions as a significant factor in helping us maximise our time. Your choice of companions is crucial. Knowing who you are will help you in choosing your friends and optimising your teenage years.

Reflection:

What are you doing with your time?

_____

_____

_____

_____

_____

_____

_____

Would you say that you're wasting time, spending time or investing time?

_____

_____

_____

_____

_____

_____

_____

Do you have a personal timetable for home use?

_____

_____

_____

_____

_____

_____

Do you think that time is nonessential, that you can do whatever you like with it?

_____

_____

_____

_____

_____

_____

CHAPTER 8

A GIRL AND HER FRIENDS

> *"If you don't know who you are, you will be someone else. That is why we conceal our true selves and wear the image of others. We bear their brand. If you don't have your own unique identity, you will adopt the brand of another." –* **Sunday Adelaja**[35]

I believe you can now see that you have the power within you to be exactly who you want to be. It does not matter what anyone else thinks; you can decide your own Identity and it is essential for you to find yourself. The only way you can become you and avoid adopting anyone else's image is by discovering yourself. Your ability to honestly be you will determine the quality of relationships you have.

> *"One's friends are that part of the human race with which one can be human."–* **George Santayana**[36]

Your friendships are significant. I had lots of friends when I was in secondary school and some of those people are still my friends, even now that we are grown adults with families of our own. Some of the friendships you make in secondary school will last a lifetime, while others will fizzle out. However, you are going to be making connections with others – boys and girls. You will need to pay close attention to who you choose to have as friends. Your friends could either be a blessing or a curse to you. They are vital to you as a teenager and as a young adult. as they give you that sense of belonging that you need. However, there are some things you need to remember about making and keeping friends.

Hey, girl! I want to remind you again : for you to be able to have successful relationships and involvement with others, you need to find yourself. "If you don't know who you are, you will be someone else."

No one was created to be a copy of another. We were all created to be unique. Everything that makes you different and unique was in your DNA at your conception! That doesn't change, even if you were born as an identical twin. Scientists say that we are so unique that no two people's fingerprints – of the billions of people on earth – are ever the same. [37]

You are just so beautiful the way you are.

You are a unique design.

A unique brand.

You are a masterpiece!

There is no one just like you on the face of the earth. The One who created and designed the universe and all humans called you perfect and blessed.

Hey, girl! You should be feeling good about yourself right now! You are you, and there is no one else like you, and that is the truth. You are an original!

> *"We are each gifted in a unique and important way. It is our privilege and our adventure to discover our special light."*— **Mary Dunbar**[38]

Having this awareness is crucial as you begin to make friends and associate yourself with others. No one really wants to be an imitation. However, as young people, we seem to forget this. You forget who you are and suddenly want to be like someone else instead. It could be your friend or someone you saw on social media or TV. You want to speak like them, dress like them and even think like them. The more you do this, the more you gradually begin to lose yourself and become someone else.

> *"You were born an original work of art. Stay original always. Originals cost more than imitations."- Suzy Kassem.*[39]

Positive and Negative Influences (Peer Pressure)

Friendships will always affect us positively or negatively. One major issue you will face as a teenager is that of peer pressure. The people you choose to be involved with will either make you better or make you worse.

As teenagers, it is only natural to want to hang out with your friends. You want to do things and go places together. I remember having my friends visit me at home when I was a teenager. My mum was very welcoming and accommodating of them. I would visit them too. However, I had different types of friends. There were friends to have a laugh or chat with. There were also friends who I was close to because they were my relatives or lived in the same neighbourhood. And the other group of friends I had were those that I studied with or who helped me with revising difficult subjects or completing challenging homework. So yes, you can have different categories of friends. This all depends on what you want from your friendships And who your friends are. Remember, not everyone can be your friend. Teenagers are quick to form cliques at school so they can belong to a particular group of friends. The question you must ask yourself is: what kind of girls do you have in your circle?

I was never in a clique when I was a teenager, but I saw them at school. Most of them were particular about dressing up the same and wearing the same shoes or hairstyles. They were usually very noisy and were good at talking about others and making fun of those who were not up to their standards. Some of them were bullies because they thought they were better than others. They even got into the habit of fighting with other girls to intimidate them. Are you in a clique? It's okay to have a regular group of friends. That's not a clique. A healthy group of friends doesn't try to stop you from having other friends. A healthy group of friends allows you to act like yourself. A healthy group of friends accepts you for you.

Do you bully others? If you are bullying, it's time to stop. You are not only hurting someone else; you could hurt yourself. You can lose friends and get in trouble with your school or even with the police. If you can't seem to stop yourself from bullying, get help from an adult you trust. You can make friends with those who challenge you to study or do good things, or you can become friends with those who will influence you to despise doing good and get you to waste your time and fall into trouble.

Hey, girl! Who you choose to associate with is your decision and it's a big one.

When I was a teen, some girls were serious and focused on school, but others were busy talking about boys and other unimportant things. I remember a clique of girls leading another student to her boyfriend's house after school. While they were there, another boy raped her. It was a setup, but she went with them because she wanted to belong. I also found myself in a difficult, unwelcome situation when I was younger. A classmate of mine came visiting to my house and wanted us to go visit her boyfriend. I didn't have a boyfriend then. When we got there, they were dancing, and there was this other boy that groped me and tried to get me to dance with him. I decided I would never go with anyone for that kind of visit again.

Where do you go with your friends? Some of your friends may get you in trouble if you are not careful. They could also become a distraction for you. I remember telling my mum to tell my friends that I was sleeping so I wouldn't get distracted from doing my chores or schoolwork. Do you have a way to avoid getting distracted by your friends? You can come up with a secret code with your mum or another friend to get their help with escaping from people you don't want to spend time with. As teenagers, our friends are essential to us, but we must be careful about how we choose friends. Make friends with those who motivate you to do better. Avoid friends that do not want to take their life seriously. Remember, your time is your Life. Do not waste it for the sake of friendships.

Respectful Relationships

One important thing about friendship that I would like to mention is RESPECT. Respect is about treating ourselves and others with dignity and consideration and respect should be an essential factor in every relationship you have.

What is a Respectful Relationship? This type of relationships allows you to feel valued and accepted for who you are. Respect is a vital part of your physical, social, sexual and emotional development.

In respectful relationships:

- You can make your own decisions and choices and each person is treated equally and fairly.

- You can point out one another's mistakes.

- You are only intimate when you both want to be. You agree that you'll have sex only when you're both ready and there's no pressure.

- You know it's okay to say no to sex, alcohol and anything else that makes you uncomfortable and your peers will not put pressure on you.

- You communicate openly and sort out conflict fairly. For example, if you disagree about how much time to spend with each other, you can look at your commitments together and come up with a solution that works for both of you. In this way, you're respecting each other's time.

Disrespectful Relationships

In disrespectful relationships, you are *not* treated with dignity or consideration and are pressured to do things you are not comfortable with. Here are some signs for recognizing a disrespectful relationship:

- They try to control you and always tell you what to do.

- They blame and humiliate you or use emotional blackmail. They may even be verbally abusive.

- They're physically abusive. They may even call it playing.

- They're sexually abusive. They trick or force you into sexual activities. You may not understand that what's happening is abuse or that it's wrong, and you might be afraid to tell someone about it. Sexual abuse can happen anywhere—and it can occur in person or online.[40]

Hey, girl! Are you in a disrespectful relationship?

Think about it. Be wary of people who do not treat you with respect. Some will even follow or harass you, either face-to-face, by using technology to repeatedly text you, demanding to know where you are, or by spying on you when you are out with other friends.

All of these behaviours show disrespect, and you should not maintain a relationship with anyone who behaves like this. It is not compulsory to associate with others; it is a choice you make. Choose your friends and loved ones wisely. Do not let anyone make you do anything you don't want to do or make you go where you aren't comfortable.

At the beginning of this chapter, I mentioned that if you do not know who you are, you will end up becoming somebody else. Know yourself, value yourself and respect yourself. Until you can do these things, you will not have healthy and respectful relationships.

Be willing to end any friendship that is not doing you any good. You don't really need it.

There is a famous saying by Vladimir Lenin that goes like this: *"Show me who your friends are, and I will tell you what you are."*[41]

I believe you will now be able to see the importance of choosing sound associations and being in respectful relationships. Don't live in the shadow of anyone else. Be your own kind of girl!

Reflection:

Who are your friends right now?

_____

_____

_____

_____

_____

_____

_____

What kind of influences do your friends have over you?

_____

_____

_____

_____

_____

_____

_____

Do you feel valued and respected in your relationships?

_____

_____

_____

_____

_____

_____

_____

_____

Are your relationships respectful or disrespectful ones?

_____

_____

_____

_____

_____

_____

_____

CHAPTER 9

DARE TO BE DIFFERENT

> *"Being different is one of the most beautiful things on Earth. Embrace your "you' ness." - A. Edwards*[42]

I mentioned in the previous chapter that it is vital for you to know who you are, so you don't end up becoming who you are not. I must emphasise again that the people you associate with will either have a positive or negative influence on you. As humans, we are all created for relationships. As long as we are here on earth, we will always need one form of companionship or another.

As teenagers and young adults, one major issue you will have to cope with is the need to belong. The need to belong is the reason that cliques form. In a bid to keep up with friends, we find ourselves trying to be like them. We dress, talk and even copy behaviours and mannerisms that we think are cool. A lot of girls lose their own identity and unknowingly take on the someone else's character. It is okay to admire others and be inspired by their achievements and successes but to be just like them is not possible.

In the over 7,5 billion people on planet earth, there are no two who are precisely the same, not even if they are born as twins. *Everyone* is different, and although people can be quite alike sometimes, there's always at least one thing that makes them who *they* are and differentiates them from others. You are a unique being. A masterpiece! To live in this reality and accept your differences is very important. If everyone were the same, the world would be a boring place.

When bullies go after your looks and differences, it means they have nowhere left to go. And then you know you're winning!

"I have Asperger's syndrome, and that means I'm sometimes a bit different from the norm. And - given the right circumstances - being different is a superpower." —Greta Thunberg.[43]

There is a reason why you were created different to others. If everyone were the same or tried to conform, they would not be useful to society. It's only when we truly embrace who we are that we make an impact.

Why am I emphasising difference? Because, a primary reason for depression, self–harming and suicidal thoughts stems from the fact that young teens feel they are different from their peers.

There is nothing wrong with being different. Maybe you are not as tall, slim or intelligent as the next person, but think of the things that make you unique. What are the things that you can do that they can't? Do not despise the things that make you different from others. Those are your strengths. Instead of looking at others and wishing you were like them, look to yourself and pay attention to the things that set you apart.

Don't shy away from being different and don't put yourself under pressure to do what your friends are doing just because you don't want to feel different. If you can't embrace your difference, you will end up doing things you will regret.

Dare to be different, even if it means you are left alone.

Dare to have a mind of your own and stay true to yourself.

Do not let anyone make you do things you don't want to do just so that you can belong. Don't go smoking or drinking just because your friends are. Don't go to somewhere your friends knowing that your parents will not approve. Many people have made these mistakes and live in regret today. They wish they had stayed true to themselves.

I used to ask myself all these questions as a young girl: Why am I different to my family? Why am I not like my friends? Why am I a part of this particular family? Why was I even born in this country? Why am I not as intelligent? Why am I not as beautiful? Why is my family not like that family? These are just some of the questions that come to mind when we begin to notice our differences. Maybe you are already asking yourself these questions too. Do you know what begins to happen as you ask these questions? You begin to lose your confidence and your sense of worth. This is the basis for low self-esteem. However, if you understand that your difference is good, you will embrace it.

Your differences don't mean you don't deserve to be respected, honoured and celebrated. Your differences are telling you to believe in yourself. The ways you are different are where you deserve to be celebrated. These are the springboard for you to jump to success. Are you different in any way? Then be confident about it.

Your differences are Divine. Your peculiarity and your nature is all divine. How you look and how you talk all comes from God. You are who you are by God's will, so who can argue with that?

Hey, girl! Do not let anybody put you down, humiliate you or talk down to you. Your differences are your superpower!

What are your gifts or talents? What do you like that others don't? All of these things also point you to your uniqueness. They show that God has His hand on you. Others only celebrate those who celebrate their own differences. If you notice that you are different—in the way that you sing, dance or cook, then improve on it and perfect it. Soon others will celebrate you. Don't try to hide or change yourself. People will praise your uniqueness, not your fleeting beauty. Your beauty will change, but who you are will endure.

Self-confidence is knowing yourself and being at peace with your differences and your uniqueness. You must know you are special. It is not about being *better* than somebody else, it is about being the best version of you. Your difference is what makes you unique. Celebrate it! Embrace it!

"Don't Try To Be Someone Else You're Not, Else You Miss Out On Who You Truly Are." – Anonymous[44]

When you know and believe in the worth of your differences, it gives you energy.

> *"Embrace your difference. You are most comfortable being you. You can only perform better when you embrace who you are. Your point of difference is your point of relevance."* — **Sunday Adelaja**[45]

We are all different from one another. In your difference is your glory. Dare to be different!

Now that you know that difference is good, what must you begin to do?

1. Take note of the things that make you different from others.

2. Develop your uniqueness. Enhance and emphasise it. Add value to what God has given you.

3. Develop your talents. Maybe you sing or draw very well, or you are a good athlete. Develop these skills even more.

4. Look for where your difference is in demand. Look for those who celebrate and welcome your differences.

5. Find opportunities to serve with what makes you unique. Use them to make a difference and to be a blessing.

6. Honour and appreciate other people's differences. Part of self-confidence is being able to celebrate both yourself and others.

What about Disabilities?

Maybe you have a disability, and you are thinking that it is nothing to celebrate. Well, I would like to tell you that you are beautifully made and Marvellous.

Hey, girl! Your disability is not a curse. It is the platform for your greatness. Don't allow anybody to put you down for it.

Here are examples of some people who did not allow their disabilities to limit them:

Jessica Cox (born 1983 in Arizona) is the world's first licensed armless pilot, as well as the first armless black-belt in the American Taekwondo Association. She was born without arms due to a rare congenital disability. She is able to use her feet to drive an unmodified car and type on a keyboard at 25 words per minute. She is also a certified scuba diver. She is able to pump her gas and put in and remove her contact lenses.[46]

Another person who had attained greatness despite few accommodations for her disabilities is **Helen Keller.**

Helen Keller is the first person to have earned a college degree while being blind and deaf. The play and film *The Miracle Worker* show various parts of Keller's life that include the way her teacher, Anne Sullivan, developed a language that Helen could easily understand. Helen successfully wrote 12 published books, including her autobiography. In it, she says,

> *"Although the world is full of suffering, it is also full of the overcoming of it".*[47]

This is so true. We can overcome obstacles. They should not be allowed to limit us or stop us from accomplishing our goals.

Marlee Matlin is another successful disabled woman. Marlee is a Deaf Academy Award and Golden Globe-winning actress for her portrayal in the movie *Children of a Lesser God*. She has been on many TV shows and reality shows. She says,

> *"It was the ability that mattered, not the disability, which is a word I'm not crazy about using".* [48]

Having a disability should not restrict you. It should instead challenge you to achieve and overcome the world's lack of accommodations so that you can make it accommodate you. When you understand this, you will know that impossible is nothing!

Body Image

Body image has to do with how we think and feel about our physical selves, and how we believe others see us.

When it comes to body image, many struggle so much. You look at yourself in the mirror, and you don't like what you see. Poor body image has driven a lot of girls into taking dangerous and irreversible action. Some have even died in the process of trying to look different instead of accepting themselves. The reason for the heavy make-up, the dressing up and the cosmetic procedures some girls get into is because they do not want to embrace their differences. They want to be like someone else they saw on Instagram or on the television.

Be kind to yourself and try not to compare yourself to the many images you see online and in magazines, which are often digitally enhanced to make them look 'perfect'—they don't reflect how people look in real life. You need to be critical of social media and not allow 'perfect' videos and pictures to influence how you see yourself. Through patience, perseverance and the desire to love ourselves, we can build a healthy and positive body image.[49]

You might need to change or correct some things about yourself if they are a source of discomfort or impact your health, but do not go the route of trying to fix things that do not need fixing. Don't do things out of self-consciousness or vanity. Rather make decisions based on true need. Your teeth or a skin problem can sometimes be corrected surgically, but there are some things about us that we cannot change.

There is a viral video about Courtney Barnes, a lady from Miami in the USA, who decided she wanted a bigger butt at any cost. She started injecting her butt with substances to make it bigger. Now, she's realized that her actions could cost her life. Can you imagine that? Is it worth it? She thought she would be happy, but now she is not only sad because she knows better, she is worried about her health. She has realized that her true identity lies in who she is on the inside and wants to reverse the changes, but doctors don't think it will be easy. On top of everything, she is depressed because of all the attention she is getting about what she did.

Hey, girl! I hope you now understand why you should embrace your differences.

If Courtney had accepted herself, she wouldn't have come to this place of regret and wanting to change back. Now she is warning every girl out there not to do what she did. Courtney is now showing girls to love their bodies. Regarding cosmetic surgery, she says, "Just because it looks good does not mean it is healthy." She has made a mistake, and she is now saying, "Don't do it!"[50] The real worth is not in how you look. You are more than that!

How do you Overcome the Pressure to be Someone Else?

If you recognise your worth, you will not feel pressure to do or be who you are not. Remember, your self-confidence comes from knowing your worth. In the previous chapter, I asked 'Who are you?' If you can answer this question, no one can make you do anything you don't want to. It takes a very confident person to make it in life without being influenced. When you take a stand for being different, your peers may say negative things about you or make fun of you. Not belonging to a clique may attract criticism. However, if you know who you are, you will not be influenced by this negative criticism. Even if it means being alone, you will stand alone.

Hey, girl! What you learn will set you free.

We all have our own worth. Be confident about who you are and do not be ashamed of it or of your background. Have the assurance that you are unique and special. Your fingerprints, your eyes, your mind are all unique. You are not a mass product. Do not ever doubt that. Let this uniqueness be the basis for your self-confidence.

Affirm Yourself

Affirmations are positive statements that can help you to overcome self-sabotaging, negative thoughts. They are a proven method of self-improvement because of their ability to rewire our brains. Affirmations strengthen us by helping us believe in the potential of an action we desire to manifest. When we verbally affirm our dreams and ambitions, we become empowered with a deep sense of reassurance that our wishful thinking will become a reality.

To use affirmations, first analyse the thoughts or behaviours that you'd like to change in your own life. Then, choose statements that target these thoughts.

Here are some self-affirmations you can practice daily. You can stand before a mirror to say them. When you repeat them often and believe in them, you will start to find positive changes. You can even come up with some of your own statements to further affirm yourself and your uniqueness. Words are powerful. What you tell yourself is what you will eventually become. Speaking well of yourself all the time is *critical*. Don't put yourself down. No one will respect and value you if you do not respect and value yourself. Your self-confidence will attract others to you. Remember, it does not matter if other people like you or not. What matters is that you like yourself. Just be yourself.[51]

Love yourself and love being with yourself.

Practice saying these affirmations daily:

- I LOVE ME
- I AM MORE THAN MY FAMILY NAME
- I AM MORE THAN THE WAY I LOOK
- I AM BOLD
- I HAVE VALUABLE TALENTS
- I WAS BORN FOR A PURPOSE
- I WAS BORN TO DO GREAT THINGS
- I WAS BORN TO MAKE A DIFFERENCE
- I AM COURAGEOUS
- I AM VALUABLE

Remember to add to the list. You will be surprised at how confident you become when you affirm yourself regularly. For these affirmations to work for you, bear the following in mind:

Repeat your affirmations daily. Repetition is vital for retention.

Do it seriously. Be committed to it.

Try to feel the energy and the emotions in the words you are saying.

Write the words down and put them where you can always see them.

And lastly, believe. Believe in yourself and your affirmations, and you will see them working.

You are different: embrace it, celebrate it and never be afraid to stand proud.

Reflection:

How are you different from other people?

_____

_____

_____

_____

_____

_____

_____

_____

Do you feel comfortable in your differences?

_____

_____

_____

_____

_____

_____

_____

_____

Do you wish you were like somebody else?

List the things you like about yourself and why you celebrate them.

CHAPTER 10

MAKE A DIFFERENCE

> *"If you desire to make a difference in the world, you must be different from the world."—**Elaine S Dalton**[52]*

What does it mean to make a difference? It means to cause a change, to be important in some way.

It also means to do something remarkable, to do something that helps people or makes the world a better place.

It's critical to note that people who've made a real difference aren't all privileged, advantaged or "important" by any stretch. Many come from disadvantaged families, crushing circumstances and initially had limited capabilities where they were, but they have all found ways to pick themselves up and rise above their circumstances to transform their own lives and the lives of those around them.

Here are some more examples of young people who have made a difference around the world:

Zuriel Oduwole is the youngest person of African descent to find a place in the "100 Most Influential People in Africa" list. What did she do to achieve this? At just ten years of age, she became the youngest person to be profiled by Forbes Magazine for screening a self-produced movie commercially. She has already made five documentaries.

By the time she was sixteen years old, she had already become an education activist filmmaker who's showing the positive side of Africa. She has travelled to 11 countries through her side project "Dream Up, Speak Up, Stand Up" and talked to about 24,000 children about the importance of education, particularly girls' education.[53]

Another young teenager who is making a difference is **Hania Guiagoussou**. A junior at Dublin High School in California, she is changing the world through her apps. Using her coding skills, she has developed projects with great social impact. One of these projects is WaterSaver, an app that gives users the ability to monitor and control their water sources from anywhere.[54]

Patricia Manubay was a victim of bullying in elementary and middle school. To help other kids achieve their dreams, she started thinking outside the box. She launched her project "Dream Boxes" at the Jefferson Awards 2015, in New York City, "to get children and students the supplies and resources they need to be successful in school, as well as the support and empowerment they need to make their dreams happen."[55]

Another beautiful story is **Meghan Markle's**. She is the Duchess of Sussex and a member of the British Royal family now. When Meghan was just eleven years old, she had to assess the messages of various adverts for a class project. The advert for Ivory dishwasher soap caught her eye because of its gender-specific language. The voiceover said, "Women all over America are fighting greasy pots and pans." The young activist-to-be found offence with the use of the word 'women.'

With encouragement from her dad, she wrote letters to the soap's manufacturer, Procter & Gamble, as well as to civil rights lawyer Gloria Allred, Hillary Clinton (who was First Lady at the time) and Nick News anchor Linda Ellerbee. Due to her letters, the advertisement's wording was changed, replacing "women" with "people." [56]

All of these young people are just like yourself, making a difference in one way or another. These shining examples are proof that you are never too young to make an impact. I want to end with this quote from Ralph Waldo Emerson:

"The purpose of life is not to be happy. It is to be useful, to be honourable, to be compassionate, to have it make some difference that you have lived and lived well."[57]

In the next chapter, you will see how our differences shape our values and how you can focus on developing your values. You will learn more about why it is so crucial for you to be yourself and not be like anybody else.

Reflection:

What are your gifts/talents?

_____

_____

_____

_____

_____

_____

_____

Are you able to stand alone when everybody else is doing the same thing?

_____

_____

_____

_____

_____

_____

_____

How are you making a difference—at home, at school and in your community?

_____

_____

_____

_____

_____

_____

_____

_____

CHAPTER 11

A GIRL AND HER VALUES

> *"I have learned that as long as I hold fast to my beliefs and values, and follow my moral compass, then the only expectations I need to live up to are my own." –Michelle Obama*[58]

O ne important trait to possess if you want to be different and achieve your dreams is having uncompromising personal values. Staunch personal values are essential to have if you're going to succeed, fulfil your dreams and maximise your life as a young person. Value, according to the Oxford English Dictionary, is defined as the regard that something is held to deserve; the importance, worth, or usefulness of something. [59]

Your values, therefore, are the things in life that are important to you. Maybe you have not yet started thinking about this. However, now is the time to start thinking and making a list of your values. An essential adage that stayed with me as a teenager myself was,

> *"If you don't stand for something, you will fall for anything." —Peter Marshall*[60]

Our values are what we should live by, but sadly, many people do not. When you live by your values, you will feel better about yourself and be more focused on doing the things that are important to you.

Why do Personal Values Matter?

Personal values are the characteristics and behaviours that motivate us and guide our decisions. For example, honesty may be of value to you. You believe in being honest and speaking your mind. Anytime you are dishonest, you feel disappointed in yourself. Or maybe you value kindness. You like to be nice to others and help them in whatever way you can.

Those are just two examples of personal values. Everyone has their own values, and they can be quite different. Some people are competitive, while others value cooperation. Some people value adventure, while others prefer security. Some may have negative values like selfishness and greed.

> *"Values are like fingerprints. Nobody's are the same, but you leave them all over everything you do." —Elvis Presley*[61]

Values matter. They tell you how to live. You're likely to feel better if you're living according to your values and to feel worse if you're not. Personal values apply both to day-to-day decisions and to more significant life choices. Defining your values and then living by them can help you to feel more fulfilled and to make choices that make you happy, even if they might not make sense to other people.[62]

My studies were critical to me when I was a teenager and all through my years of education. As a result of how much I valued studying, I kept a personal timetable as I've mentioned before. The timetable was to help me focus on my studies daily. I always felt happy when I knew I had met my goals for the day, according to my timetable.

I also value kindness. I want to help in whatever way I can anywhere I find myself. My ability to help others fills me with a sense of happiness and fulfilment. I feel terrible when I am not able to help as I would like. When I go anywhere, I ask myself: What can I do to help here? If I find something, I go ahead and do it.

How do you define your values?

You may first want to ask yourself, What makes me feel good? You may also choose to ask yourself what makes you feel bad. Positive and negative emotions can help us with determining our values.

Personal or moral values are essential as you journey into adulthood. Moral values are sets of principles guiding us to evaluate what is right or wrong. Moral values help shape character and personality.[63] As children growing up in Nigeria, we were taught moral values in the form of folk tales or stories. Today, you find some of these values in films like *Brave*, which teaches courage, and *Frozen*, which shows the power of love.

Where have you learnt about values?

Examples of the values that you can choose to embrace and develop as you grow into adulthood are:

- honesty or dishonesty,
- love or hate,
- hard work and diligence or laziness,
- self-confidence or self-doubt,
- personal responsibility or irresponsibility,
- respect for others or disrespect for others,
- self-control or impulsiveness,
- kindness or wickedness,
- forgiveness or grudge holding,
- cheerfulness or moodiness,
- reliability or unreliableness,
- loyalty or disloyalty,
- commitment or lack of commitment,
- open-mindedness or close-mindedness,
- consistency or inconsistency, and
- efficiency or inefficiency.

Which values will you choose to embody? Think carefully about this.

Are any of the above-listed values already a part of you?

Every person should inherit certain core values such as integrity, determination, loyalty and respecting others. As stated earlier, values help us distinguish between what's right and wrong and good or bad for you as well as for the society around you. As a result of adopting positive personal values, your decision-making power improves naturally. Respecting each other, no matter the age of the person standing in front of you, helps you gain good relationships with people from every walk of life. You'll have good relationships with family, in the workplace, and with others in your society. Adopting positive values also helps you find the real purpose of your life. For many girls, the lack of personal/moral values has led them to live a life of regret. They have not been able to distinguish between right and wrong, and some have lost their lives for this.[64]

"A highly developed values system is like a compass. It serves as a guide to point you in the right direction when you are lost."
— Idowu Koyenikan[65]

Values are essential in life for the following reasons:

- Values help you differentiate between good and bad.
- Values reflect an individual's character and spirituality.
- Values help in building good personal and professional relationships.
- Values can help in eradicating problems like dishonesty, violence, cheating and jealousy.
- Values counter the ugliness of society like disrespecting women, child abuse, violence and crime.
- Values help you deal with tough situations. They can be crucial to staying self-motivated.[66]

Develop your own Personality

Your values will determine the actions you take. They will also decide whether you will become a dynamic personality or just another face in the crowd. To stand out and succeed in life, you need to define yourself by your values. Values fill your life with meaning. hey are like magnets: they attract either good or bad people into your life. Take the famous musician Amy Winehouse, for example.

Amy Winehouse started her music career at the age of sixteen but by twenty-seven, she was dead. Why? Her story is a clear example of someone who was living without values. Even though her music was winning her a lot of awards, Amy was developing a reputation as an unstable party girl. She was drinking and soon got addicted to drugs. She was also in an abusive relationship. She often overdosed on drugs and had to be admitted into hospital for treatment. I police once even arrested her for possession of marijuana. She briefly went to rehab, but Amy couldn't stay sober. Her lack of control and values saw her destroying herself, even amidst her popularity. Though she was the first British singer to win five Grammy awards, Amy's lack of values led to the deterioration of her health and personal life. At the end of her life, no one was talking about her musical success. She is not remembered today as a musical personality so much as she is of a woman whose life was destroyed by an addiction to drugs and alcohol.[67]

Had Amy Winehouse clearly defined her values, do you think she would have lost herself to drug addiction?

Do you want to be an unremarkable girl without values, or a dynamic personality? If you are a girl with no values, you will easily allow the crowd to move you. You will want to do what everyone else is doing for fear of missing out (FOMO) even when you know that going with the flow may hurt you. You will quickly forget yourself and who you are if you are without values.

On the other hand, you can't be easily influenced by the crowd if you hold onto values. A girl with values is confident in herself and can make her own decisions without being a puppet in someone else's hands. Such a girl is a personality. A personality never compromises their values. For you to be a personality, you must:

- withstand pressure from others and from the difficulties of life,
- live by your goals and your purpose, and

- continue to develop yourself through self-education.[68]

Hey, girl! I hope you now understand why having personal values are essential. Remember, for you to maximise your life, you need values.

The meaning of your life will depend on the values you cultivate within yourself. Don't deprive the world of your gifts and talents because of a lack of values. Develop and hold onto your core values.

In the next chapter, we will be discussing some of the ways you can begin to maximise your life

Reflection:

Write out five values that you identify as being yours.

_____

_____

_____

_____

_____

_____

_____

_____

How would you explain this phrase: "Values are like fingerprints. Nobody's are the same, but you leave them all over everything you do"?

_____

_____

_____

_____

_____

_____

_____

_____

How would you use it to describe yourself?

_____

_____

_____

_____

_____

_____

_____

What do you think are the consequences of a lack of values in a person's life?

_____

_____

_____

_____

_____

_____

_____

CHAPTER 12

HOW TO MAKE THE MOST OF YOUR YEARS

> *"Live your life on purpose with no apologies or regrets."*
> *—Angela Cecilia* [69]

Now that we have seen how critical personal and moral values are, I would like to share some more secrets to making the most of your life as a young person with you. In previous chapters, I emphasised why this phase of your life is significant and why you *should* make the most of it. We are born as helpless babies, we grow up and grow old, and then we die. Many may not even grow old before they die. Life is an opportunity, and we need to make the most of it. Nobody has the promise of tomorrow. Every day that we wake up is a gift, and we must appreciate it as such. The sooner you start building the life you want, the easier it will be to appreciate this gift of life.

> *"It is good for people to submit at an early age to the yoke of His discipline."* *-The Bible* [70]

This time now is for you to build your life. Remember, one misconception adults will have about you as a teenager is that you are not capable of taking responsibility for your life. We now know those misconceptions are not valid. Many young people like you are doing great things already.

When I was a young person in the 1970's and 1980's in Nigeria, nobody told us to dream or pursue our personal goals. For most girls, we waited for our parents to tell us what they wanted for us. Whatever else it was they wanted for us first, the ultimate goal always ended in getting married and giving them = grandchildren. Life is not just about good grades and jobs, getting married and having children. We are supposed to live our lives with a purpose. We are meant to live life to the fullest, and maximise our full potential. For many girls, the lack of awareness that life has much more to offer has made them unable to maximise their possibility. Some were fortunate enough to realize their dreams and pursue them after having children and even in old age. But for you, you don't have to wait and struggle to accomplish the things later when you can accomplish them now if you are focused and maximise your years as a teen and young adult.

Hey, girl! You are at the best phase of your life to begin building the life that you want. If you pay the price now, in making an effort, you will have so much joy and fulfilment in the future. It does not matter what comes your way, you will know that you lived life to the fullest and did not waste your time on earth.

Here are some more self-development tools that you can begin to use to make the most of your years as a teen or young adult.

Develop Self-discipline

One of the secrets to maximising your life as a young girl is to develop self-discipline. Self-discipline is "the ability to control yourself and to make yourself work hard or behave in a particular way without needing anyone else to tell you what to do." It is synonymous with having self-control or self-restraint. Being disciplined gives you the strength to withstand hardship and difficulties, whether physical, emotional or mental.[71] Self-discipline is one of the cornerstones of living a successful and fulfilling life and is something we should all strive to master. When you train yourself to do the things you should *when* you should do them, you will enjoy the following benefits:

- You will achieve your goals quicker.
- Your self-esteem will soar.
- People's respect for you—especially your parents' and teachers'—will grow.
- You will influence the lives of others, your siblings and friends especially.

- You will see greater success in all areas of your life.

- You will enjoy a more rewarding and satisfying life.

On the other hand, when you consistently neglect things you know you should swiftly, these are the effects:

- You won't achieve your goals. I've never met anyone who lacked discipline and achieved anything worthwhile .

- You won't feel good about yourself. No matter how hard you try to justify your actions, you know what's right and wrong. Lying to yourself will only make it worse.

- You'll lose the respect of those who are dependent upon you and your actions.[72]

Many adults today are living a life of regret because they refused to be disciplined when they were younger. Some people have even lost their lives due to a lack of self-control and are not here to tell their stories.

Hey, girl! It takes discipline for you to get to the peak of your game.

"We must all suffer one of two things: the pain of discipline or the pain of regret and disappointment." —Jim Rohn[73]

Be a disciplined girl. Study when you should, even if you don't feel like it. The decision to be disciplined is the best decision you can make. I want to challenge you to start doing all the little things you know you should do. Focus on your gifts and talents and practise more. As you do these things, reward yourself for each task. With constant awareness and sustained effort, you can train yourself to become disciplined.

"The distance between your dreams and reality is Discipline." —Unknown[74]

Keep Reading, Keep Learning

If you want to make the most of your time now, you must understand the importance of reading. There is plenty of time for you to read at this stage of your life. Instead of watching TV, gaming or spending time on your phone—*Read*, girl!

> *"The more that you read, the more things you will know. The more that you learn, the more places you'll go." —Dr Seuss* [75]

Hey, girl! It is crucial for you to keep reading and learning new things. A reader today is a leader tomorrow.

Here are some benefits of reading:

- Reading develops your mind and creates new neural pathways in your brain. Your mind is a muscle, and it needs exercise.

- Reading is a tool for communication. It is one of the essential tools we use every day to connect with others and with the world at large.

- Reading allows you to discover new things. By reading, you can gain experience from other people and avoid their mistakes which will hasten your achievement of a goal.

- Exploration begins with reading and understanding.

- Reading develops your imagination and creativity. Books train your imagination to think big. With reading, a person can go anywhere in the world—or even out of the world entirely! You can be a king, an adventurer or a princess. The possibilities are endless. Non-readers never experience these joys to the same extent.

- Reading prepares you for action. Maybe you want to learn to cook a meal or read the menu before ordering a meal. Anything you want to do that requires help and guidance, reading will prepare you for it.

- Reading improves your understanding. The more you read, the more you understand. Reading can also help you find the truth. It even increases your knowledge of the rules of life so that you can adapt and accommodate society better.

- Reading plays a role in self-improvement. It helps you form a better you. Through reading, you will begin to understand the world more. Through reading, you will begin to have a greater understanding of topics that interest you, such as how to build self-confidence, how to make a plan better before taking action or how to memorise things more easily. All of these self-improvements start with reading.[76] Reading is fundamental for developing the right self-image. Non-readers or poor readers often have low opinions of themselves and their abilities.[77]

Reading is essential because words—spoken and written—are the building blocks of life. You are, right now, the result of words that you have heard or read and *believed* about yourself. What you become in the future will depend on the words you think about yourself now. Words have been used to build people, families, relationships and even nations. Think about it…

"I do believe something very magical can happen when you read a good book." —J.K. Rowling[78]

Acquire New Skills

Your time as a young person is the time for you to acquire skills. Don't run away from any opportunity to learn just because it is hard. Keep learning. Be curious and interested. You can manifest your potential and discover yourself far more when you are open to learning. Take advantage of every opportunity to learn something new. It could be a sport, vocational skill or gardening. It could even be a computer or technological ability, like coding. Whatever it is, the more you expose yourself to a variety of new activities and skills, the more you will be able to find the things that come naturally to you. These are the things you will enjoy and will be able to dedicate yourself to fully. If it is singing, you will be able to take music classes so you can improve. It could be playing tennis or running. Whatever it is, so long as you are open to learning, you can become decent, if not the best, at it. Never shy away from any opportunity to learn something new and gain a new skill.

I am grateful for the opportunity I had learning to sew because my mum was a seamstress and we had sewing machines at home. I also learnt baking and pastry-making from my aunt. We often went to visit my cousins and spent a lot of time joining them in helping their mum with her baking business. I learnt how to make cakes, pies and other pastries. I also learnt how to make ice-cream from an older friend—Auntie Rose, we fondly called her. Making ice-cream was a skill I used to make money when I was a university student. As an adult, the ability to bake became useful for me when I couldn't return to work after having my first baby.

My son was born with special needs, a condition known as Osteogenesis Imperfecta (Brittle Bone Disease). He needed a high level of care, and we constantly had to go into hospital with him. Having the skills to bake meant I was able to work from home And I now run my own food production company. What if I hadn't had any skills? It would have been so much harder to begin learning something new as an adult with a baby to look after. Now, while you are young and free, gain all the skills you can from this self-development toolkit. Remember, you will not have this level of freedom when you get older. Use your time well. You never know when some of the things you are learning now may be needed. Life is an opportunity! Success comes when preparation meets opportunity.

"Do the one thing you think you cannot do. Fail at it. Try again. Do better the second time. The only people who never tumble are those who never mount the high wire. This is your moment. Own it."
—Oprah Winfrey[79]

Accept Responsibility

To make the most of your years, you will need to be responsible. Accepting responsibility also means being accountable. This attitude of responsibility begins first at home. How reliable are you at home? As a young person, you don't always see the long-term effects of your behaviour. However, the only way to gain the respect and admiration of those around you is to accept responsibility. Accepting responsibility is usually two-fold: personal responsibility and indirect responsibility.

Personal responsibility is taking ownership of your behaviour and the consequences of that behaviour. Until you accept responsibility for your actions and failures, it'll be challenging for you to develop self-respect let alone have the respect of others. We all make mistakes and poor choices sometimes. We all have had times when we fail to do something we know we should be doing. You will not be the first or the last person to falter in your behaviour. We all fail sometimes. Failure is learning. Don't be afraid to try again when you fail. In every failure is a lesson of how not to do something the same way again. If someone is hurt by your actions, then accept responsibility by apologizing and do all you can to make amends. It would be irresponsible of you not to do so when you are in the wrong.

Indirect responsibility involves moving beyond yourself and taking action to help people or improve situations around you. While this may not rise to the level of personal responsibility, it does reveal something about your character and the type of person you are. Many people will walk right by litter in the corridor at school. However, there are others—thankfully—who will quickly pick it up and bin it. It is not difficult to choose which of these two actions is the more responsible behaviour.

Accepting responsibility, personal and indirect, is one of the most critical factors in defining a person's real character. When that moment of responsibility comes, what you do—or don't do—is an indication of the type of person you are.

Failing to accept personal responsibility may work to your advantage on occasion in the short term. For example, you might get away with keeping your mouth shut about something that you've done, or even blaming someone else for your misdeeds. You might not promptly face the consequences for your actions. But make no mistake about it, this poor choice will catch up with you eventually, and it'll typically cause more pain for you down the road than if you'd stepped up and taken responsibility initially.

> *"When you blame others, you give up your power to change."*
> **—Author Unknown** [80]

Unfortunately, many teenagers today are always looking for someone or something to blame for their mistakes. Blaming someone else is a serious matter, and there are consequences when you choose not to accept responsibility-. In the long run, you will have no one to blame but yourself.

One of the consequences of not accepting responsibility is the effect it has on your mind and heart. When you know you have failed to take responsibility for something that you should have, it'll begin to bother you, to eat at you, little by little. Pretty soon, you'll feel tiny inside. Life functions better when you take responsibility for your actions. You will never be able to gain the respect of others when you are known for not accepting responsibility. There's a good chance that when you avoid taking personal responsibility, someone will see that you've failed in this way. In other words, someone else may know that you're responsible for the wrongdoing or poor choice, and when they see you fail to accept responsibility, they'll lose all respect for you. If this happens frequently, you'll never gain the respect of others.

> *"Accepting personal responsibility for your life frees you from outside influences increases your self-esteem, boosts confidence in your ability to make decisions, and ultimately leads to achieving success in life."* **—Roy T. Bennett** [81]

Hey, girl! Accept responsibility for what you do and the choices you make. Begin to practice personal responsibility now.

I learnt to take responsibility by making sure I carried out any given task or chore at home and school. As you grow into an adult, it will be easier for you to gain respect and be given responsibility at home, at school and in any other field you find yourself in if you begin to practise accepting responsibility now. Be a responsible girl.

> *"In the long run, we shape our lives, and we shape ourselves. The process never ends until we die. And the choices we make are ultimately our responsibility." —Eleanor Roosevelt*[82]

Be Prepared

Preparation is the key to success. Do not leave your life to chance. Always be prepared. Being able to learn new things and to keep learning will help you to live a prepared life. You never know when an opportunity might come knocking at your door. You may have big dreams and goals and the perfect plans, but if you fail to prepare, it doesn't matter how good your ideas are, or how beautiful your thoughts are, you will fail.

> *"I believe luck is preparation meeting opportunity. When opportunities come, you wouldn't have been lucky, if you lack preparation." —Oprah Winfrey*[83]

As a young person, you may be academically inclined or into sports or music. Or, you may have another unique talent or gift. How are you preparing academically and in your other areas of interest? You do not have to wait for examination time to start studying. You do not have to wait for a competition to practise and improve in sports or art. You can begin making plans now knowing that the test or game will eventually come. Preparation will save you from a lot of stress and anxiety. How are you preparing for your goals and dreams? Even though it is usually common to do so, do not neglect planning. Preparation is one of the critical things we need to do when planning for or looking forward to something. There are several benefits to being prepared.

Being prepared helps you to start well. When you make preparations, starting well is easy, because you have put some measures in place before starting.

It also helps you understand what you still need to do. With preparation, you have an understanding of everything that you will need for a particular goal or course of action. With this understanding, you can identify some key areas to modify or replace.

Being prepared also helps you to know the strengths and weaknesses of something. Through preparation, you have an understanding of the strengths and weaknesses of an action you are planning to undertake. Also, you have an idea of how you can use this knowledge to your advantage. [84]

As a young person in education, one thing I learnt to do was not to study a day before any examination. I used the day to rest and make sure I had everything I needed to take my exams. I ate well and slept well in order to arrive early at my destination. Preparation will help you to do this. Do you have a dream of being a singer, actor or professional athlete? Begin to make plans for realizing that dream now.

*"Success is where preparation and opportunity meet." —**Bobby Unser**[85]*

Work Hard

Hard work is related to preparation. There is no success or achievements in life without hard work. We only succeed to the degree of the effort we are willing to put into our task or endeavours. It doesn't matter how gifted or talented you are; without hard work, you will become a failure in life.

"Hard work beats talent when talent fails to work hard."
— Kevin Durant[86]

Nobody is great without work. Working hard is always the baseline for great achievements. Nothing spectacular comes without it. Very few have ever failed with the hard–work approach to making it in life. You may rise slowly, but you are sure to improve. As a young person still being educated, hard work is essential for you to succeed in your studies. Apart from your studies, it is also necessary that you work hard on anything that interests you or any talent that you may possess. If you don't work hard, you will never get to the top.

Serena Williams, one of the world's most talented and inspiring tennis players, said "Luck has nothing to do with it. I have spent many, many hours, countless hours, on the court working for my one moment in time, not knowing when it would come."[87]

There are no shortcuts to lasting success, only *smart* cuts. Many people will do what's most comfortable and avoid hard work—and that's precisely why you should do the opposite. Lasting success is only achievable if you put in the work. Hard work is challenging, painful and uncomfortable. But it's the only way to the top. One of the keys to success is to learn to enjoy working hard at a challenging task. I remember how poor I was at maths. I was always failing, as I could not understand my maths teacher. I knew I had to work hard. During the holidays, I met with an older cousin of mine so she could teach me. She was excellent at maths. I left my friends and the comfort of my home to begin studying with her. I didn't have time to play around. This decision paid off. By the time school resumed, I had become so good at maths that the teacher would refer those who did not understand a topic to me. Can you believe that? I am still not the best at maths, but I know enough to not be scared of the subject anymore.

You have probably heard this phrase a hundred times, "you have to work smart, not hard, to succeed." Being smart is about making the right choices. Intelligent people move up the ladder fast. *But* they also value the importance of hard work. Your idols, heroes, and every other successful person you know worked hard and made essential and calculated choices before they reaped the rewards of success. As they reached the pinnacle of success, they grew more experienced, made fewer mistakes, improved their decision-making skills and made the most of opportunities. The result is that they are able to save a lot of time, effort and energy. You can only give something your best shot and work hard towards your goals. Don't see failure as an obstacle. Rather, be smart enough to learn from it.

The good thing about hard work is that it's universal. It doesn't matter what profession or career you want to get into,hard work can be used to achieve positive long-term results for you.[88]

In the words of G. K. Nielson, *"Successful people are not gifted; they just work hard, then succeed on purpose."*[89]

Hey, girl! Don't run away from hard work. Most people don't recognise opportunities because they come in the form of hard work. You will keep missing opportunities if you are not willing to work hard. You are born to do hard things, and you are capable of doing them. Hard work pays off.

Now that you know the secrets to making the most of your life as a young person, I urge you to take them seriously and begin to apply them to your life. Start building your life and create the experience you want. You will be amazed at how you will stand out, in *any* environment you find yourself in.

Reflection:

What is your attitude towards these things?

- discipline,
- reading,
- learning new things,
- accepting responsibility, and
- hard-work.

Which of these stands out the most for you?

_____

_____

_____

_____

_____

_____

_____

Which of these do you need to work on more to make it a part of you?

_____

_____

_____

_____

_____

_____

_____

_____

What are three things you could do to become more responsible?

_____

_____

_____

_____

_____

_____

_____

CHAPTER 13

THE PRINCIPLE OF DELAYED GRATIFICATION

> *"The ability to discipline yourself to delay gratification in the short term to enjoy greater rewards in the long term is the indispensable prerequisite for success."—Brian Tracy[90]*

The previous chapter showed you how important it is for you to have discipline, learn new things, accept responsibility and work hard. As important as these things are, you may still end up with regrets if you do not also apply the principle of delayed gratification.

Wikipedia defines gratification as the pleasurable emotional reaction of happiness in response to a fulfilment of a desire or goal. Gratification usually comes in two forms; it is either instant/immediate or delayed. [91]

Instant gratification is the desire to experience pleasure or fulfilment without delay or deferment. It's when you want it, and you want it now. Instant gratification is the opposite of delayed gratification. Waiting is hard, and there is an innate desire to have what we want when we want it, which is usually without any delay. Social media and advertisement have increased the desire for instant gratification. Here are some examples of instant gratification:

- The urge to eat unhealthy fast foods and snacks instead of cooking foods which contribute to good health.

- The desire to keep sleeping instead of waking up early for school or classes.

- The temptation to go out for fun with your friends instead of finishing a paper or studying for an exam.[92]

- The temptation to go out for fun with your friends instead of getting a good night's sleep on a work night (which is one temptation that crosses generational boundaries!).

- The desire to buy something on credit, like a phone instead of saving until you can afford it.

- -The urge to spend all your time with a new boyfriend instead of working towards your long-term goals.

You have probably noticed that at least one or two of these examples apply to you. Not all instant gratification is bad. There's nothing wrong with wanting or needing things, experiences or products on time, but it is essential to balance our desires with a realistic sense of timing and patience.

Delayed gratification, on the other hand, refers to the ability to put off something mildly fun or pleasurable now to gain something that is more fun, pleasurable or rewarding later. For example, you could watch TV the night before an exam or you could practice delayed gratification and study. The latter would increase your chances of getting an A in the course at the end of the school year, which is much more satisfying in the long-term than a night of watching TV.

> *"Don't give up what you want most for what you want now."*
> *—Richard G Scott[93]*

Why is it vital for you to have this ability to wait? You already know what delaying gratification entails, which means you already know how difficult it is. We want whatever it is now, and we usually do not like waiting. No one does.

Babies seek immediate gratification, aiming to satisfy cravings such as hunger and thirst, and find whatever they want in the moment to ease their discomfort. Babies are usually not able to delay gratification. When a baby cries, it is generally for immediate gratification. It is either for food, a nappy change or sleep. The baby will not be able to wait. Until you meet the need, the baby will keep crying.

As the baby gets older, there will be times when waiting is necessary before a requirement is met. Maybe the parent may request that the child tidy up first before getting an ice-cream or have a bath before dinner. Your ability to develop this habit of waiting will determine how well you can delay gratification later on in life.

If you are someone whose parents always give you anything you want without making any demands of you in return, then this will be hard for you. However, if you are willing, you can develop this habit and live a fulfilling life.

> *"I believe the sign of maturity is accepting deferred gratification."*
> *—Peggy Cahn*[94]

A well-known study conducted at Stanford University in the 1960s explains a lot about why it's beneficial to delay gratification. In the study, children were placed in a room with one marshmallow on a plate. The lead researcher gave the children an easy instruction: You can eat the marshmallow now, or wait 15 minutes and receive two marshmallows. The researchers found that the children who were able to wait for the second marshmallow without eating the first one scored higher on standardised tests, had better health, and were less likely to have behavioural problems. [95]

Delayed gratification can be harder for people from certain economic backgrounds to practise, though it is just as important. Everyone can practice delayed gratification.

Consider the results of this study and think about yourself and your actions.

- Are you able to wait for things you want, even if it involves sacrificing pleasure and satisfaction now?
- Do you make decisions based on your life's purpose or on what feels good right now?
- Do you sometimes give up too soon?
- Can you think of a time when you accomplished a difficult task?

- How did it make you feel about yourself?
- What were the results of waiting?

Studies show that delayed gratification is one of the most common personal traits of successful people. People who learn how to manage their immediate need to be satisfied thrive more in their careers, relationships, health and finances. Over time, delaying gratification will improve your self-control and ultimately help you achieve your long-term goals faster. Here is an example:

Zain Asher, a CNN news anchor, gave a talk at TEDxEuston where she told the story of how her mother stopped her from watching television for eighteen months so she could focus on her studies and go to Oxford University. Her story is an example of delaying gratification. Zain said, "I was only allowed to watch BBC and CNN international. If I was to watch anything else, I had to ask special permission for that". No television expanded to no phones, no cable and no music. "I had nothing else to do but study," she said. She didn't find this so easy at the time but she trusted her mum and gave up her phone and television. Television and phones will always be there. She could always come back to them after her exams. She is now glad she listened to her mum as she was able to go to Oxford, and now has her dream job as a CNN anchor. [96]

I cannot emphasise developing the skill delayed gratification enough. You may be wondering how you can do this. It is not easy to go to the sports club, studio or music club to practise when you know your friends are hanging out just chatting and having fun somewhere else. It is not easy to stay awake to get your assignments done when you can go to sleep instead. For you to be able to do these things, you must be able to delay the gratification of fun or rest. You can develop this quality with practice. The ability to delay gratification is critical for success in life.

If you delay the gratification of watching television and get your homework done now, then you'll learn more and get better grades.

Success usually comes down to choosing the pain of discipline over the ease of distraction. And that's exactly what delayed gratification is all about. If you want to succeed at something, at some point, you will need to find the ability to be disciplined and take action instead of becoming distracted and doing what's comfortable. Success in nearly every field requires you to ignore doing something more comfortable (delaying gratification) in favour of doing something harder.[97]

As a young person, your primary goal is your education. You must be focused on your goal to get the reward of good results at the end. The pressure from your friends and the desire to have fun and hang out all the time will present itself often. You can choose to delay satisfying this desire and focus on your goals. There will always be time to hang out with your friends and have fun. You will not be in school forever.

Hey, girl! Set your priorities straight and take charge of your own choices. Don't let someone or something else dictate them.

How to Practice Delayed Gratification

Even if you don't feel like you're good at delaying gratification now, you can train yourself to become better just by making a few small improvements. We can train ourselves to delay gratification, just like we can train our muscles in the gym. The key to learning to delay gratification is in creating an environment in which you reward yourself. You can do this by promising yourself a treat later if you do X, Y and Z and then actually follow-through.

Tell yourself you can buy that new pair of shoes after you put in 100 hours of study time, and then actually buy them if you manage it.

Tell yourself you can treat yourself to your favourite food after you have completed two workouts this week, and then actually eat the pizza.

Each time you assign a task and follow through, you are training your brain and teaching it that delaying gratification is a good thing.

Another way of practising delayed gratification is to use it to build new habits. Find something even mildly rewarding that you already do and determine how to reward yourself after you perform it. For example, if you want to read more books, tell yourself you will watch your favourite Netflix show after reading five pages. After a while, you'll find that delaying gratification becomes a habit in itself and you'll be accomplishing more meaningful things in your day-to-day life because of it.[98]

"The longer you have to wait for something, the more you will appreciate it when it finally arrives. The harder you have to fight for something, the more priceless it will become once you achieve it. And the more pain you have to endure on your journey, the sweeter the arrival at your destination. All good things are worth waiting for and worth fighting for." — Susan Gale[99]

You can now understand the importance of delayed gratification and why you should make it a part of your life. Waiting is good sometimes, and it will bring greater rewards in the future. In the next chapter, I will be sharing with you how having all of these qualities that I've mentioned in the last two sections can help you to avoid common problems and risky behaviours that young people often find themselves in. If you want to make the most of your life and live without regrets in the future, then you need to pay attention to these secrets.

Reflection:

Why do you think it's essential to delay gratification?

_____

_____

_____

_____

_____

_____

_____

Can you identify instances when you've delayed gratification?

_____

_____

_____

_____

_____

_____

_____

Are you able to focus on your studies even when you feel like just being on social media?

_____

_____

_____

_____

_____

_____

_____

You have to submit your homework tomorrow, but your favourite TV show is on. You know you can watch it at another time. What do you do?

_____

_____

_____

_____

_____

_____

_____

CHAPTER 14

SEX, ALCOHOL AND DRUGS

> *"You should save the best part of yourself for the person who deserved you." —Anonymous[100]*

In the previous section, I took a lot of time to help you understand the necessity of making delayed gratification a part of you if you want to make the most of your life. A significant setback for many young girls is the overwhelming desire to belong. You want to be loved and accepted and, as a result, you make poor friends and even go to the extent of forming cliques. The fear of missing out (FOMO) has caused many girls to get involved with friends who are more like enemies (frenemies). Your success in life is determined mainly by your environment. The need to be in the right environment is the reason why the people you spend most of your time with and the places you hang out at matter a lot.

As we draw close to the final chapters of this book, I want to bring your attention to some common problems found among teenagers. The good news is that the vast majority of young people like you will not be involved in any of these risky behaviours. However, these are common issues among young people that you *must* recognise. Indulging in these risky behaviours will have a significant impact on your life in the future.

Hey, girl! The purpose of this book is for you to recognise your worth and to make the most of your life as a young person. I want you to know that you can also become an achiever and become great at your young age. It's not too early for you to achieve greatness. You can do it! Now is the time to lay a strong foundation for your life. Now is the time to build your experience. Now is the time to be focused, pursue your dreams and become all that you were created to be.

Your life as a girl–child is so important and so different from that of a boy. Society still has many unfair expectations of the girl–child. For this reason, you need to grow up strong and equipped to stand up as a personality that is not defined by gender, but by results. It is vital to get your bearings right in life and become a self-sufficient young lady. You were born to do great things, remember that.

Sexuality

Sexuality is a part of who you are and who you'll become. It's not just about sex. It is about how you:

- feel about your developing body,
- make healthy decisions and choices,.
- understand and express feelings of intimacy, attraction and affection for others, and
- develop and maintain respectful relationships.

Your personal experiences, upbringing and cultural background influence your beliefs and expectations about sex and sexuality. Whatever your values and beliefs are, I want you to be aware of safety, responsibility, honest communication and respect which must be found in any sexual relationship.

It is typical for young people like you to want to experiment with sexual behaviours. Experimentation is a healthy, natural and powerful urge. But not all of your relationships include sex. As you grow physically, you are maturing emotionally and socially too. You might want romantic intimacy and other ways to express love and affection. And you might be curious and want to explore adult behaviour. Some girls are sexually attracted to people of the opposite gender, some to people of the same sex, and some are bisexual. Sexual attraction and sexual identity aren't the same. Young people who are attracted to the same sex might or might not identify as gay, lesbian or bisexual. They might identify as heterosexual. [101]

Even though I did see different sexual orientations growing up, it was not very common back in the day. Nowadays, it has become common, and you need to be aware of it.

I began to get attracted to the opposite sex when I was about twelve or thirteen years old. It was an older guy who I was suddenly crushing on. I believe it was in response to my changing body and the hormones that were playing an active role in my development. All I wanted was for him to notice me. I wanted him to talk to me. I would sit outside my house, just waiting for him to walk by and say hello. Maybe he was shy or perhaps he didn't even notice me, but after a while, that feeling faded. Thinking back now, I am glad he didn't notice me at all. I was putting myself at risk. Most teenagers usually put themselves at risk because of the urge to express and receive love and affection. Unlike you, I didn't have any education about sex and sexuality then. It could have all gone wrong. I could have been taken advantage of and abused. The truth is I wasn't ready to handle the feelings I was having, and no one was talking to me about them.

You are not your Vagina

Why do I say this? As you grow up, you will have sexual attractions, and they are healthy. In a society that is highly sexualised, many people of the opposite sex often see girls as a sex object. When people see you as this, they begin to hunt you as prey. I want you to know this. There are lots of good people out there, but there are also some that are bad. It is often challenging to identify predators. It is *often* those who you trust and respect that want to take advantage of you. You need to recognise that you and your body deserve respect. Do not allow anyone to pressure you into having sex, drinking or doing drugs. Sometimes your closest friends could be used as bait to lure you into sex, drinks and drugs. Holding onto your values is vital here. What are your values? Have you defined them? Are you portraying yourself as a sex object? You will get the attention, but not respect. Remember what we said about delayed gratification? There is a time for everything. Don't rush into having sex with just anyone.

Know your Worth

If you don't know your worth, you will be seen as a sex object and become trapped in a mess that will be challenging to escape. A girl without boundaries will become a girl without respect. You set the standards for how you want others to treat you. You're a Marvellous Girl! It's not about pride but about value.

Just because someone desires you doesn't mean that they value you. No matter how good looking they are or how exciting they seem, you are worth so much more than someone who is playing games with you.

> *"It is better to be alone and wait for what you deserve than lower your standards and settle for less than God's best for you."*
> *—Brittney Moses.* [102]

I remember going out with some friends, and one of them had her boyfriend with her. We went into a café for drinks, and the guy ordered alcoholic beverages for everyone. I objected and requested something else as I don't drink alcohol. My friends tried to say that I should try it as I was not the one paying anyway. I refused. And at that moment, I realised I shouldn't be hanging out with this lot. They were not respecting my choice but wanted me to do what they were doing instead. Anyway, I got my own order and after that day, I never went out with that particular girl again.

Hey, girl! I know your friends are a big deal to you. However, choose your friends wisely. Recognise those that you share common values with and stay away from friends that do not share your values. Do not hang out with the wrong company simply for fear of missing out. Above all, seek *respect*, not attention. Respect lasts longer.

Sexting, Cybersex or Nudes

These terms all describe the act of sending naked pictures or videos of yourself to a friend, via a mobile, using a webcam, or on social media. None of these are ever private. Once a photo is shared, you have lost all control of it, and it will be virtually impossible for you to take back. Even if you change your mind and delete the photo you uploaded, other people may have already shared or copied it. Sexting puts you at risk of abuse or exploitation by others.

According to a report by the UK's NSPCC (National Society for the Prevention of Cruelty to Children) survey:

- on average, one child in every primary school classroom in the UK has received a nude or semi-nude image from an adult, and

- one in 50 school children has sent a nude or semi-nude picture to an adult.[103]

Sending photos or videos of yourself to people you don't know is dangerous. Any explicit communication with people you don't know is terrible. Sometimes abusers will pretend to be your age. You may think you're sexting with people you see as your friends and people you can trust. The truth is, anyone you send a photo to can take advantage of you for doing it—even people you know in real life, including so-called "friends" in your year group.

Abusers will flirt with you, flatter you and make you feel exceptional—all to earn your trust and make you think they are your friend. They will start conversations with you about sex and convince you it's good to talk to them about it. If you're feeling down or unloved, they will boost your self-esteem and try to earn your trust. But the truth is you can't trust them. They are exploiting you and abusing you, but by the time you realise this, it may be too late.[104]

Hey, girl! It is foolish to think that it cannot happen to you. Be safe when you're online!

You've already read about how to handle your relationships with your friends in the previous chapter. Be careful of those you choose to be your friends. Don't hang out with friends that try to make you do bad stuff. There are lots of evil people out there, and you need to be careful. Some of the places you go with your friends may end up being traps. Most people today get into trouble because of the friends in their lives.

Hey, girl! Don't be naïve. Trust your gut and follow your heart but take your brain with you. If it doesn't feel right, it probably isn't.

According to formal statistics, one in five women has been abused sexually. [105]Yes, you read that right. And unfortunately, the offenders are usually not strangers. People often think that in most cases of rape, the offender is a stranger, but the truth is the majority of people who commit this crime know their victims and are relatives, friends or work colleagues.

It is essential to know these facts:

- You have the right to say NO. All young people have the right to control what happens to their bodies, and you should never feel pressured into doing anything that doesn't feel right. You should not just be doing what your friends are doing. NO MEANS NO!

- "Safe sex" means protecting against both pregnancy and sexually transmitted infections. You can do this by using condoms if you are sexually active. Having said this, re-member the principle of delayed gratification. Sex is fun, and it should be a pleasurable experience, but it comes with responsibility and consequences. Remember too that no method of protection is 100% effective.

- If you are sexually active, then you must get tested for STI's, especially chlamydia. This condition is usually symptomless and is very common in young people of both sexes.[106]

- You can get advice about sexuality and sexual health from several places, including your GP/ doctor. You can also ask your parents or other trusted adults, like your mentors or teachers, anything you want to know.

Think about what you do and don't know and get as much information as you can. Don't be shy to ask questions and find out information. Read! Don't be ignorant. Don't be misled by social media and put yourself in harm's way. Sex is good and powerful. It is to be enjoyed and not abused. There is a time and a place for it. Don't expose yourself to sex before you are ready to bear the consequences and the responsibility that comes with it.

> *"So many young people find things such as sexy dancing and dressing provocatively now wholly acceptable, yet are completely unaware of some of the risks this behaviour can come with, especially when you show it over the internet. I firmly believe this is due to the portrayal of celebrities in the media. I think many young females feel that if a star can dress or act in a sexualised way in front of millions of people in the media, then it must be acceptable for them to do the same."*
> *—Abi – 17 years old* [107]

When you dress and act sexually, you are sending the wrong signals, and people can take advantage of you. You are not the way you look or dress. Don't make yourself a sex object.

Hey, girl! You are worth so much more. **You** are here for a purpose, and the whole world is waiting to see the greatness that you have inside. Do *not* reduce your life to sex, drinks and drugs. "Save sex instead of safe sex."

Adverse Effects of Early Sex, Alcohol and Drugs

Studies have shown that when you engage in early sexual intercourse, it can result in some of these common problems:

- an increased risk of having multiple sexual partners in your life time,
- sexually transmitted infections (STIs),
- unwanted pregnancy,
- problems with orgasm and sexual arousal, and
- depression and low self-esteem.

All of these have a way of making your life confusing and less fulfilling. You don't want your experience to result in dealing with unwanted pregnancy and STIs or low self-esteem because it happened too early. Sex is beautiful and it is worth the wait. Do not get involved in casual sex. The negative consequences that come with it are not worth it. Respect yourself enough to know that you deserve the best. Do not allow yourself to be manipulated and abused. When it comes to sex, save it for someone who truly respects and deserves you, someone with whom those feelings are mutual. You are worth it!

If you are ever assaulted, know that it is not your fault. Rape can happen with anyone, either in the family, among those you call friends or people in authority above you. Don't keep quiet about it! It does not matter if anyone believes you or not. Speak out and get help. See a psychologist and get counselling. Rape is traumatic and you shouldn't have to keep it to yourself. Keeping it secret will do you more harm than good. You don't have to suffer for the wrong someone has done to you. You can get help and begin to heal. You don't have to live with the pain of being violated. You can find love and be loved by someone who truly respects you and deserves to be in your life.

Grooming

I would like to make you aware of grooming. Maybe you already know the word—I never heard it growing up. According to the United Kingdom's National Society for the Prevention of Cruelty to Children (NSPCC), "Grooming is when someone builds an emotional connection with a child to gain their trust for sexual abuse, sexual exploitation or trafficking. Children and young people can be groomed online or face-to-face, by a stranger or by someone they know—for example, a family member, friend or professional."[108]

You may be being groomed and not even know it. If you are not careful, you could quickly become a victim. Someone (male or a female) may be buying you gifts and being so lovely to you just so that they can control you or abuse you sexually. If it does not feel right, don't accept it. Many young people—because they come from a low-income family, or so they can belong to a clique—are easily tempted. Maybe you want to do what others are doing or want instant gratification. However, this often ends badly. Be wary of people who are older than you always buying you gifts and wanting to take you

141

out on trips or give you attention and advice. These could be close family members like uncles and aunties, a boyfriend or girlfriend or even a religious figure if you belong to a religious group. They may be grooming you. Once they know you trust them, they may take advantage of you.

A famous case is that of the Rochdale child sex abuse ring in 2012 which involved underage teenage girls in Rochdale in Greater Manchester, England. Nine men were convicted of sex trafficking and other offences including rape and conspiracy to engage in sexual activity with a child. Forty-seven girls were identified as victims of child sexual exploitation during the police investigation.[109]

There's a story on the internet about a girl who went out with her friends to a party and never returned. Her name is Kenneka Jenkins and she was nineteen years old. She was found dead in a freezer in a hotel in Chicago, USA. Social media platforms like Facebook and Twitter shared the alarming story. Many people believe that her friends left her to be assaulted and violated by a group of men. A video of Jenkins and her friends in a hotel room went viral and this raised the suspicions as to what could have happened to her. The men are suspected to be involved in trafficking and rape. Her parents are distraught, not knowing what happened to their daughter and her friends are too scared to disclose what happened. One of then tried to commit suicide instead of telling the truth.[110]

Online grooming is even more dangerous. Many stories abound on the internet of girls who fell victim to online grooming. Many girls are being abused, and some have even lost their lives. Here is one of them:

> **'Naomi'** said, *"I was good at sport at school. And my family was what you would call 'normal'. I met Nick on the internet and thought he was in his mid-twenties. We got on well and agreed to meet up. As soon as I saw him, I knew something was wrong—he looked about fifty!*
>
> *"I'd invited him to my house when my parents were out, and it was clear he was expecting sex or something.*
>
> *"I felt like I'd led him on and didn't know how to say no, so I agreed to have sex with him. I immediately regretted it and*

told him I didn't want to see or speak to him anymore. But he wouldn't leave me alone and kept trying to get in touch. I didn't know what to do so I told a family friend and the police got involved."

The police identified the man in Naomi's story as a local businessman. When they seized his computer, they discovered that he had been chatting to other underage young people, telling them he liked 'young girls'. He frequently tried to meet up with the people he chatted with for the explicit purposes of having sex with them, even though he knew they were not yet 16, which is the legal age of consent.[111]

You can never be entirely sure of the identity of those you chat with online. It's not okay for you to chat with strangers. Be safe online.

I have said a lot about sex. Now, let's look at drinking, smoking and drugs. These are risky habits you don't want to get involved in. It all comes down to your values and those you hang out with. If you keep company with friends who drink, smoke or do drugs, the likelihood is that you will join them sooner or later.

Alcohol is an addictive substance that your body absorbs into the bloodstream from the stomach and small intestine. The liver slowly breaks it down like it does any other toxin before your body eliminates it.

In general, the liver can break down the equivalent of about one drink per hour. Nothing can speed this up, not even black coffee. As alcohol reaches the brain, you'll start to "feel" drunk. This feeling varies from one person to the next and from one situation to the next.

In all situations, alcohol depresses the brain, meaning it slows down the brain's ability to control the body and the mind. This effect is one reason why alcohol is so dangerous. Have you seen someone under the influence of alcohol or drugs? Was it a pleasant sight?

"Drunkenness is nothing but voluntary madness."—Seneca [112]

Alcohol is the most commonly used addictive substance in the world. If you make careless decisions regarding alcohol, you may face severe consequences, including possible jail time, suspension of your driver's license, injury or even death.[113]

Drugs are dangerous. Make informed decisions if you have to choose whether to accept a substance or turn it down. There are many illegal drugs out there and, because many of these drugs are new, little about the effects of taking them has been made known. Many of these drugs are manufactured in home labs with no quality control standards. What this means is that, at the very least, dosage levels may vary from dose to dose and additional harmful ingredients may have been added. Recently, videos of some of the effects of these new drugs have gone viral on social media.

Taking drugs can be dangerous—not only because of the physical toll they can take on your body but because they can also reduce your ability to set limits, be aware of your environment and realise when you are in danger. Because there are many risks involved with using drugs, it's best to obtain information about them now and make an informed decision before you place yourself in a situation where you will have to choose in a hurry to take a drug or turn it down.

Hey, girl! Do not be deceived into thinking that it's fine to try it and nothing will happen to you.

What happens when you take drugs is that your brain produces chemicals that allow you to feel emotions like happiness, pain, anger and depression. Some drugs contain the chemical that causes a feeling of extreme euphoria. As you take more pills, your brain receives so much of this "happy chemical" from the drug that it starts to create less of it naturally.

Therefore, without drugs, you always feel unhappy; you then need the drug to feel joy. You are compelled to take more to attain that feeling as you become immune to its effects. After a while, low-scale drugs like marijuana will no longer provide you with the pleasure you need, and you will find yourself yearning for more—moving on to more dangerous drugs such as crystal meth and cocaine.

This creates an addict. Why are drugs so detrimental? They result in a chemical process that you cannot control. Your life should never be out of control, but sex, drinking and drugs can make a wreck out of you.[114]

Hey, girl! I am sharing all of this because I do not want you to be ignorant and naïve. Your teen years are fun, frustrating, exciting and even a little scary. Navigating all the changes can be hard. Don't make it worse by experimenting recklessly and engaging in risky behaviours.

Many young lives like yours have become damaged beyond redemption as a result. Their dreams and their great potential have been destroyed. While some were able to recover and start over again, the truth is that years have been lost and it is never easy to start again, even with a lot of support. Many still live with regrets for their lost years.

Set your priorities straight. Take charge and be in control of your life. There is power in your ability to delay gratification when it comes to sex, drinking and drugs. Practise the wait. Learn to be patient and focus on the things that matter now. The whole world is waiting for you. The world is your oyster. Don't limit yourself and your dreams by being impatient. Don't be a part of the negative statistics. Focus on your goals and dreams and pursue them. I am rooting for you because I know that you have greatness inside of you.

Albert Einstein said, *"If you want to live a happy life, tie it to a goal, not to people or things."* [115]

I believe you are now able to appreciate how risky behaviours can make us waste the most productive time in life. Don't live for the now, for instant gratification. Instead, think about your dreams and the future. Put your imagination to work. In the next chapter, we shall be discussing family relationships. Families are an essential part of our lives.

Reflection:

What are your beliefs regarding sex, drinks and drugs?

_____

_____

_____

_____

_____

_____

Remind yourself of your dreams and goals again. Are they worth losing for the sake of sex and drugs?

_____

_____

_____

_____

_____

_____

Have you been assaulted? If yes, did you speak to anyone? (You should never be quiet if someone has abused you sexually. It has far-reaching complications on your wellbeing. Speak out until someone listens.)

There are resources listed at the end of this chapter for you to get help, if you need it.

CHAPTER 15

YOU AND YOUR FAMILY RELATIONSHIPS

> *"There is no doubt that it is around the family and the home that all the greatest virtues… are created, strengthened and maintained."*
> —**Winston S Churchill**[16]

I mentioned in the last chapter that our environment, especially our family traditions and culture, has a significant influence on our attitudes and beliefs about sex and sexuality. Most of our values come from what we learn and observe in our families, whether good or bad. How we relate to our families can help us as we grow up into young adults.

Family is one of the most important, if not *the* most crucial, thing in our lives. We all come from different family backgrounds. Having healthy relationships with your family members is both important and challenging. Without our parents, we would not be here in the first place. We need our parents, but sometimes they may not be there.

Families in the 21st century come in all shapes and sizes: traditional, single parent, blended (more than one family together in the same house), and gay and lesbian parents, to name a few. No matter the "type" of family you have, there are going to be highs and lows, good times and bad. [117]

Maybe you are living with only one of your parents, or you are with a guardian or carer or even in foster care. Whatever the circumstances right now, the truth is, you need an adult in your life—someone you can look up to, that is responsible for you.

However, I do realise that some young people like you have had to take responsibility for their own lives as a result of not having anyone there to be responsible for them. If you are in this situation, you still need someone to look up to. It could be a teacher at school, an aunt or uncle or someone in your community. We are all created for relationships. You can reach out to an adult you respect and ask if they can be your guardian or mentor. You must also commit to listening to and respecting them. If the adult is not willing, don't be discouraged. Be patient. You can reach out to another adult until you find someone who will be there for you. Don't be afraid to ask.

Good family relationships benefit you by:

- making you feel secure and loved, which helps your brain develop,

- helping you overcome difficulties with your eating, sleeping, learning and behaviour,

- making it easier for you to solve problems and resolve conflict,

- helping you respect differences of opinion as you develop more independence, and

- giving you the skills you need to build healthy relationships of your own.[118]

It can seem like there's a "perfect family" Ideal. But different families face different issues, including: divorce or separation, moving homes, excessive arguments, abuse or neglect, drug or alcohol problems, domestic violence, money worries, and cultural differences. No matter what you and your family are going through, you're not alone.

Many times, our family relationships may be blocked by hurt, anger, mistrust and confusion. These emotions are natural and healthy and there are few families who do not have at least a few experiences with them. The worst time for most families is during a divorce.

Our relationships are vital, and this is why it is worth looking at the relationships you share with your parents and other family members and thinking of ways to improve them.

Don't be Self-absorbed

A self-absorbed person cares only about themselves and their own needs. You probably know some people who always talk about themselves, make every issue about themselves, and are generally all about "Me, me, me!" People like that are called self-centred: as the word suggests, they only focus on themselves. Self-absorbed people tend to ignore the needs of others and only do what's best for themselves.

Hey, girl! For you to have great family relationships, you cannot be self-absorbed. If you live your life as if everything is about only you…, you will be left with just that: only you.

Don't be a self-absorbed girl. Ask yourself these questions: What difference are you making in your family? Do you wait to be told what to do all the time before helping out at home? There is always something you can do to help out. There are lots of other teenagers like you who help their parents. Be concerned about others in your family. The world does not revolve around you. Mutual sharing and active listening is an essential part of any healthy family relationship and every other relationship too. Nobody likes a self-centred person. Try to think of others and what they may be going through. Be willing to make compromises. Don't always make yourself a priority. As you are growing into adulthood, you will need to show more maturity and not be selfish like a young child.

Your parents or guardians are doing the best they can for you, probably juggling work, friends, household management and more. You can always look for ways to help them. It is never too late to begin the process of improving family relationships—even if they are already of good quality—by developing some simple skills. Your family will likely be a constant presence in your life, so when an argument or issue arises, it may seem impossible to handle. But it's not.

Communicate

Remember that communication is key to resolving conflict. While it may seem that your siblings are always around to annoy you or boss you around, they are also there to communicate with. Use your family's presence to your advantage. Communicate with each other, develop ways to value boundaries, and build trust and respect.

It can be challenging if your family argues a lot, if your parents have divorced or separated, or if your parents have drug or alcohol problems. But talking to your parents or carers is a critical step in having good relationships with them. And talking can make a complicated relationship better. Sometimes it's easier to talk about the little things. You could start by telling them something about your day or asking them how their day was. Such conversations can help you connect more and make a relationship a little bit easier. It may also help your parents learn how to be there for you if you go through a difficult time. Don't isolate yourself from your family. "Family gives you the roots to stand tall and strong."

Whoever you are and whoever your family is, you deserve to get the things you need. If you aren't getting basic needs, like food and clothes, this is neglect. Ask an adult for help if you are being neglected. You can talk to a teacher at school or to a friend's parent. And remember, you can always speak to a counsellor.

If you are feeling unhappy or if someone is hurting you, get the support you need as soon as possible. You could call the police or you could talk to an adult you trust to report the neglect or abuse.

Is Running Away the Answer?

Some young people feel that running away may be their only option. But there are always other options out there. You could face worse problems if you run away and end up on the streets. Life on the streets is tough. You could be raped, exposed to alcohol and drugs or even be killed. It's the same if you run away from problems at home to an older boyfriend in the hopes that he will take care. Maybe he *will* welcome you and let you move in. Still, many girls who did this do not have great stories to tell. You could be abused, impregnated or left out on the streets again. Even if your boyfriend is decent, you will struggle to finish your education or make anything of yourself. If you must leave your home, talk to another adult you trust who may be able to help. Don't just go out onto the streets.

Every relationship requires compromises to survive, whether it is a husband-wife, brother-sister, parent-child or even master-pet relationship. If you find yourself in a difficult or abusive situation, don't make an impulsive decision which may harm you. Don't run away. Living on the streets is very hard. You'll be cold, hungry and in danger. You might face problems like:

- having nowhere safe to sleep or rest,

- not having food or clean water,

- dangerous or abusive people trying to hurt you,

- not being able to wash yourself or your clothes,

- falling ill or getting physically hurt,

- having no money,

- being attacked or having your belongings stolen from you, or

- loneliness.

Again, instead of living on the streets, always try first to talk to an adult or a teacher you trust. Ask for help and support. Someone *will* listen. You just need to keep talking. If you know someone who's run away from home, encourage them to get help for themselves. If you're still in contact with them, tell them to contact an adult, or speak to a teacher at least.

Be Accountable

The word "accountable" means to be answerable for actions or decisions and not just doing whatever you like without being responsible for your actions.

It's so easy to think you can do things on your terms because you feel grown-up. As much as you want to be independent, you still need the guidance and wisdom of those who are older than you. Don't ever be so arrogant that people cannot question you about your actions or decisions. Be willing and ready to share the reasons behind what you want to do .

> "*Accept responsibility for your actions. Be accountable for your results. Take ownership of your mistakes.*" —*Anonymous*[119]

Respect and trust are fundamental even in our family relationships. You have to give respect to get it, and respect is something everyone deserves. We need to be people who respect each other, trust and support each other and value each other's independence. Having confidence in a relationship also means proving to each other that you are reliable, responsible and dependable. The best way to be respectful is by making sure you are respecting yourself.[120] Show respect not only with your actions but also with your words. Any relationship will break down if respect, trust and accountability are absent.

Remember, life is full of relationships. If you are having a difficult time at home, reach out to others older than you who you trust and who will listen to you. Do not isolate yourself. There is always someone out there who cares and will listen to you if you reach out to them. You have a voice for a reason. Do not let your circumstances or anyone else take your voice from you. Speak out! Accept help and guidance not just from your friends but from your elders. Have a mentor, someone who can guide you and point you in the right direction. Don't forget to ask for help when you are struggling. Becoming an adult is very challenging and frightening—you need a village to support you in your journey.

Improve your Spirit

Teenagers and young adults don't often think about spirituality when they consider pushing the limits of their relationships. But spirituality is a normal part of living. Spiritual people tend to have less stress and higher feelings of well-being. Spirituality played a significant role in my life while growing up. I honestly believe my life would have been filled with a lot of pain if I hadn't embraced Faith in God very early in my life. My experience was real. I knew and believed in God's love for me and I made a decision to have a personal relationship with God: Seeking and learning and knowing Him. Developing this relationship gave me the confidence to do all that I did as a young adult. I was active at school and at church. I also led my church youth group. When I moved to another city, I got involved with the youth group there. I learnt to study and have quiet times, to develop my spirituality even more and discover myself in God and His love for me. I found acceptance and peace in knowing that I am not a mistake here on earth. There are good plans and a future for me in God's mind. This has formed the basis for my confidence.

"The best thing in life is that God sees all your mistakes and weaknesses, knows your imperfections, and still thinks you're completely amazing!" [121]

Below is a list of ten healthy ways to push your spirit to the next level:

1. Find new ways to be active in your church, synagogue or mosque. Talk with your spiritual leader about things you can do.

2. Volunteer for a community project—you'll help yourself by helping others and it makes you feel good inside. Try it!.

3. Read an inspiring book about a teenager who overcame a difficult situation.

4. Talk to your grandparents about their teenage years and what they found hard when they were growing up.

5. Spend time in nature and consider your place in the universe.

6. Learn about a new religion or lifestyle.

7. Take long walks by yourself. Become comfortable spending time with yourself.

8. Lend an ear to a friend in need.

9. Do something selfless and considerate each day.

10. Write in a diary. Writing is a way to express your thoughts and feelings. Not acknowledging your thoughts and feelings can make you physically and emotionally tense. These negative thoughts and feelings may lead to stress and illness. Negative emotions and stress can bring your spirit down. You can lower your stress hormones and relax by keeping a diary, thereby enhancing your mood.[122]

Hey, girl! Having taken the time to make you see how meaningful your family relationships are, I believe you will now begin to appreciate those in your lives who genuinely care for and support you. Never take them for granted. Love, respect and honour those who are there for you, who work to make sure you are well. Also, nurture your spirituality. Even if you think nobody loves you, I want you to know that God loves you very much. He sees, He knows, and He cares. You need to have faith and believe that God is with you and that He has a purpose and a future for you. If you seek Him, you will find Him right there where you are. Remember this.

> *"You don't choose your family. They are God's gift to you, as you are to them." —Desmond Tutu[123]*

In this next last chapter, I will be sharing some advice for you from some influential women.

Reflection:

How would you describe your family relationships?

_____

_____

_____

_____

_____

_____

_____

Is there respect and trust between you?

_____

_____

_____

_____

_____

_____

_____

Are you able to communicate freely?

_____

_____

_____

_____

_____

_____

_____

Do you feel neglected?

_____

_____

_____

_____

_____

_____

_____

If you reside in the UK and you need to talk to someone, you can call the NSPCC ChildLine - 0800 1111. If you're elsewhere, a quick internet search will help you find your local equivalent.

CHAPTER 16

FINAL
THOUGHTS
AND ADVICE

"All of us, at certain moments of our lives, need to take advice and to receive help from other people." —Alexis Carrel [124]

Hey, girl! Now that we have come to the end of this book, I would like to remind you of what I have been saying all the way through.

I am passionate about you because I believe you need to be aware of your potential and the greatness that is within you.

I want you to make the most of your teenage years and live a life without regrets.

I believe that you can take responsibility for your life and build the life that you want.

I want you to not waste this most precious time of your life, your teenage years. Make the most of this time and equip yourself with the right values and skills you need to be self-sufficient in life.

I want you to choose your friends wisely. Your friends are a vital part of your life, but not everyone can be your friend.

I want you to embrace your differences, to be you and do you.

I want you to practise self-affirmations and have faith in the power of the words that you tell yourself.

I want you to pursue your dreams, develop your values and not give in to the temptation of instant gratification.

I want you to beware of sex, alcohol and drugs. All of these come with responsibility and consequences. Don't be ignorant of the risks of engaging in these behaviours. Your dreams are worth more than any of them. Make the right choices and don't lose your focus.

I want you to not be self-absorbed. Communicate with, respect and trust those in your life who deserve it.

I want you to value your relationships and your spirituality.

I want you to live for a purpose higher than you.

> *"It's up to you today to start making healthy choices. Not choices that are just healthy for your body, but healthy for your mind."*
> —**Steve Maraboli**[125]

I have written this book to help you make the right choices and develop the correct values for your life. Life happens; things may be rough and stressful on your journey to adulthood. Your family and personal relationships may fail. However, no matter what your experiences are, I hope that this book will give you the strength and the resilience to bounce back and stand tall.

You are enough!

You are valuable!

You are courageous and beautiful!

Hey, girl! I would like to leave you with some advice that I have selected which has been given by some successful people. I hope you will take all of these messages to heart. I hope that, in those times when you are confused about stuff, you will come back here to this self-development guidebook and read through all of these to find direction and the wisdom to move on. I love you, Girl, and I am seriously rooting for you.

First, I love the advice given by Alana Wulff, the author of *Girlish*, in her post for Honey.nine.com. She advises teenage girls to look around and find someone who inspires them. It could be someone famous or someone at home. She also suggests that, when you visit your grandma, you should ask her how her life was when she was growing up. You should be friendly, kind and supportive. You should not go out with someone simply because they ask you. She advises that even though dating is fun, it is not compulsory.

Wullf also says to remember that no one thinks about your body as much as you do and says to know that no one is perfect. In her words,

"Your value is in the joy you bring to other people's lives; the books you read on the weekend when you're on your own. It's about being there for your friends and them being there for you."- Alana Wulff [126]

Here is some more advice:

Michelle Obama, former first lady of the United States:

"Walk away from 'friendships' that make you feel small and insecure, and seek out people who inspire you and support you. Focus more on learning than on succeeding—instead of pretending that you understand something when you don't, raise your hand and ask a question." [127]

Maya Angelou, poet, singer, memoirist, and civil rights activist:

"My paternal grandmother, Mrs Annie Henderson, gave me advice that I have used for 65 years. She said, 'If the world puts you on the road you do not like, if you look ahead and do not want that destination which is being offered, and you look behind and you do not want to return to your place of departure, step off the road. Build yourself a new path." [128]

Oprah Winfrey, media executive, actress, talk show host, television producer and philanthropist:

"The way through the challenge is to get still, and ask yourself 'What is the next right move?' Not think about oh I've got all of this, just what is the next right move. And then from that space, make the next right move and the next right move. And not be overwhelmed by it because you know your life is more significant than that one moment. You know your life is not defined by what someone says is a failure for you because failure is just there to point you in a different direction."[129]

Here is a collection of advice given to celebrities by others:

Kelly Clarkson, singer-songwriter:

"Sandra Bullock once said something like 'Take advice as advice.' Everyone gives you their two cents, but you have to follow your gut." [130]

Sofia Coppola, writer-director:

"When I was about 13, a friend of my parents told me always to be the age you are—don't try to seem older or younger. And I realised I was a kid trying to act like an adult, instead of experiencing my age. I've never forgotten that." [131]

Lupita Nyong'o, Oscar winner:

"Go where you are loved." Oscar-winner Nyong'o received that suggestion from the actress and playwright, Danai Gurira, and said, "It's a valuable thought that's stuck. When you're trying to find collaborators, you need to go where you are loved—because that's precisely the place where your dreams and goals will be nurtured. People who see the best in you bring out the best in you." [132]

Storm Reid, 14-year-old *A Wrinkle in Time* star:

"'Don't waste energy on things you can't change.' Oprah told me that one day when we were having a conversation about my weird fear of being tall—I'm already 5'4"! Instead of putting negative energy out into the universe about something that's set in stone, like my height, she said I should turn that energy into something positive and use it to make my dreams come true. So if I end up being 7 feet, then I'll be 7 feet."[133]

Relationship Advice

Adolescence is a fragile time filled with doubts and insecurities. There exists within you a longing for acceptance and appreciation. The major distraction for young ladies these days is relationships. Here is some advice to keep you from losing your sanity:

- Do not wait for a guy. You should spend your time discovering yourself and getting to know who you are. Don't let social media love stories and movies send you into a daydream. What if nobody ever comes or you witness a difficult relationship, will you still keep hoping for the perfect man to come by just because Cinderella got her Prince Charming?

- Do not chase a guy. You will often have crushes but that does not mean you are ready for a relationship. Losing yourself to get somebody else is stupid. Don't start putting on makeup, dressing up uncomfortably and doing other things just to impress him. You cannot fake things forever, and don't you want somebody to love the real you?

- Do not expect a guy to transform your life magically. You are enough. You don't need a guy to let you become what you want to be in life. Build yourself and pursue your dreams. Here is where actual feminism comes into play: "Be your hero and chart out the path to success." The sooner you realise this, the better your future will be.

- Do not become dependent on a guy. It's unhealthy. You may not be with him next year. Be a strong independent girl. Maintain a healthy balance between friends, family, your career, hobbies and relationships. Do you want all your memories filled with a single guy?

- Do not question yourself because of a guy. If somebody is making you feel worthless, ugly, stupid or inferior, back off immediately from that relationship before it is too late. The purpose of a relationship is to make you feel better about yourself and keep you happy. If your present relationship makes you feel the opposite, get out. Later, you will realise that you are prettier and more intelligent than he made you see yourself as.

- Do not cry over a guy for months. Let's accept that breakups hurt, and it is okay to cry over them. Once that's done, get up and think of all the bad things that existed in your relationship that you no longer have to deal. It ended for a reason, and this is how it's meant to be. Be mature and learn to regulate your emotions.

- Be strong enough to let go of any guy. Life is uncertain, unpredictable, and most things are beyond your control. No matter how strong your relationship is, it can be called off at any stage of life. Deaths, divorces and breakups are inevitable and can occur at any time. Always be a strongly independent and self-sufficient lady who can support herself, spends time pursuing her own hobbies and does not need a guy to stay happy.

Hey, girl! As I mentioned at the beginning of this chapter, I hope you will always come back here and find wisdom in the advice given. Read it all over and over again. Let it become a guiding light to you in times when you are confused. Ultimately, you get to decide. I will end this chapter with a quote by John C. Maxwell:

> *"Life is a matter of choices, and every choice you make makes you."* [134]

We have now come to the end of this journey on the amazing secrets to making the most of your life as a teen and young adult. As I end this book, I wonder if I have written everything that I want to. I realise that there is a lot more I could share, but it would make the book too voluminous to read easily.

The days when your role as a female would have been just about marriage and children are gone. "A woman's place is in the home… and the classroom, and the boardroom and the newsroom and Parliament." [135] Today, we need girls who will grow up to be:

> *"women who are so strong they can be gentle, so educated they can be humble, so fierce they can be compassionate, so passionate they can be rational and so disciplined they can be free."* **—Kavita Ramdas** [136]

You were born to win and rule.

You matter.

You are loved.

You are worthy.

You are magical.

Dare to be different.

Don't follow the crowd.

Dare to stand out.

Make no compromises that you will end up regretting. No one is you, and that is your SUPERPOWER.

Be that girl who wakes up with purpose and intent.

Be that girl who shows up and *never* gives up.

Be that girl who believes anything is possible and is willing to work for it.[137]

Be the girl who knows who she is and what she wants.

Make up your mind to succeed, and you will make your dreams happen!

"Keep your heel, head and standards high." —*Coco Chanel*[138]

Letter from the Author

Hey, girl! It has been a pleasure writing this book for you. I have been dreaming of doing this for over two years now. The desire to write this book was also the reason I founded a club for young girls like yourself, called *The Marvellous Girls Club*. The more I interacted with the girls in the club, the more I wanted to write the book as my gift of love to every young girl. No girl should be ignorant and no girl should live a life of pain and regret. Now that the book is complete and you have read it, I hope you have found every piece of advice I have shared useful. I hope you will always come back here and take the secrets from this toolkit to empower yourself. These secrets will guide you to becoming a well-equipped and confident girl on your journey to adulthood. You are worth it!

Hey, girl!

I am a girl—that girl still lives in me!

With all my love,

Grace

JOIN OUR COMMUNITY

You can connect with me and others who have bought the book on Facebook, Instagram and YouTube. I am in the group connecting with people and answering questions. It will be a great place to have me answer your questions as you read.

*Join **FREE** And Subscribe now to 'The Marvellous Girls Club' @ Facebook, Instagram and subscribe to our YouTube channel. Also, you can follow me on my Facebook page - Grace U. Anighoro*

References

1. INTRODUCTION
George Santayana. "George Santayana Quotes- A child educated only at school is an...", *BrainyQuotes*.com n.d. https://www.brainyquote.com/quotes/george_santayana_107603. (accessed December 12, 2019).

Chapter 1 – WHY AM I PASSIONATE ABOUT SUPPORTING TEENAGE GIRLS?
2. Public Health England. Local Government Association. "A framework for supporting teenage mothers and young fathers," *Digital Education Resource Archive (DERA)*. May 2016. https://dera.ioe.ac.uk/26423/1/PHE_LGA_Framework_for_supporting_teenage_mothers_and_young_fathers.pdf. (accessed April 12, 2019).
3. British Broadcasting Corporation. "Adolescent health: Teens 'more depressed and sleeping less'". *BBC*.co.uk February 28, 2019 https://www.bbc.co.uk/news/health-47390970. (accessed April 12, 2019).

4. Dr Brancho-Sanchez, Edith, "Suicide rates in girls are rising, study finds, especially in those age 10 to 14.", *CNN International*. May 20, 2019 https://edition.cnn.com/2019/05/17/health/suicide-rates-young-girls-study/index.html. (accessed June 20, 2019).
5. Catherine Pulsifer. "Regret quotes - Inspirational Words of Wisdom", *Inspirational Words of Wisdom*. Wow4u.com https://www.wow4u.com/regretquotes/. (accessed June 20,2019)

6. : Maya Angelou. "Maya Angelou quote: When you know better you do better.", *AZQuotes*.com 2019, https://www.azquotes.com/quote/346302. (accessed December 30, 2019).

Chapter 2 – THE IMPORTANCE OF YOUR TEENAGE YEARS
7. Elizabeth Gillies. "Teenage Life sayings and quotes", *WiseOldsayings*.com http://www.wiseoldsayings.com/teenage-life-quotes/. (accessed December 30, 2019).

CHAPTER 3 – THE EFFECTS OF A WASTED TEENAGE LIFE
8. Dr. Sunday Adelaja. "BECOME GREAT THROUGH THE CURRENCY OF TIME", *YouTube*. 12/14 August 24, 2016 https://www.youtube.com/watch?v=289m5-KYboE. (accessed October 20, 2019).
9. Rahis Saifi. "How Young Generation is Wasting Time on Social Media Instead They Can be Millionaire.", *HuffPost*. April 1, 2017, https://www.huffpost.com/entry/how-young-generation-is-w_b_13956272. (accessed October 20, 2019).

10. Catherine Pulsifer. "24 Choose to be happy quotes. "Being happy is something that each of us determines, it is not something that we find outside of our self, it is within us and our choice." Wow4u.com https://www.wow4u.com/happinessquotations3/", (accessed July 15, 2019).

Chapter 4 – IDENTITY CRISIS

11. Leo Buscaglia. "Leo Buscaglia Quotes - The easiest thing to be in the world is...", *BrainyQuotes*.com https://www.brainyquote.com/quotes/leo_buscaglia_150300. (accessed May 18, 2019).

12. Teresa Collins. "Quote by Teresa Collins: "You can never meet your potential until you tru…"", *Goodreads.com.* https://www.goodreads.com/quotes/7314044-you-can-never-meet-your-potential-until-you-truly-learn. (accessed May 25, 2019).

13. Malala Yousafzai. "Malala Yousafzai - Life, Quotes & Books - Biography", *Famous Biographies & TV Shows.* March 29, 2018. https://www.biography.com/activist/malala-yousafzai. (accessed May 20, 2019).

14.
Martes, Hulyo "What is the biggest misunderstanding about teenagers Today?", *Teenagers Today.* 2013 https://teenageperiod.blogspot.com/. (accessed May 22, 2019).

Chapter 5 – WHAT TYPE OF GIRL DO YOU WANT TO BECOME?

15. Socrates. "Quote by Socrates: "To find yourself, think for yourself."", *Goodreads*.com https://www.goodreads.com/quotes/26227-to-find-yourself-think-for-yourself. (accessed May 25, 2019).

16. Diana Ross. " Diana Ross quote: I can be a better me than anyone can.", *AZQuotes.com.* 2019, https://www.azquotes.com/quote/541496. (accessed December 31, 2019).

17. Jonathan Watts. "Greta Thunberg, schoolgirl climate change warrior: 'Some people can let things go. I can't.", *The Guardian.* March11,2019. https://www.theguardian.com/world/2019/mar/11/greta-thunberg-schoolgirl-climate-change-warrior-some-people-can-let-things-go-i-cant. (accessed June 10, 2019).

18. Kate Dwyer. "We Talked to Malala Yousafzai About Her College Plans, Career Goals, and Her Activism Advice.", *Teen Vogue.* April14, 2017, https://www.teenvogue.com/story/we-talked-to-malala-yousafzai-about-her-college-plans-career-goals-and-her-activism-advice#. (accessed June 10, 2019).

Chapter 6 – A GIRL AND HER DREAMS

19. Eleanor Roosevelt. "Eleanor Roosevelt - The future belongs to those who...", *BrainyQuote*.com https://www.brainyquote.com/quotes/eleanor_roosevelt_100940. (accessed June 12, 2019).

20. HARPO, INC. "Hope in a Box", *Oprah.com*. 2009, http://www.oprah.com/world/tererai-trents-inspiring-education/. (accessed April 12, 2020).

21. Steve Jobs. "Steve Jobs - Your time is limited, so don't waste it...", *Brainy-Quote*.com https://www.brainyquote.com/quotes/steve_jobs_416854. (accessed June 15, 2019).

22. . Tom Ingrassia. "10 Things I Know About Following Your Dreams", August 9, 2016. EverydayPower.com https://everydaypower.com/follow-your-dreams/. (accessed June 15, 2019).

23. headspace. "Visualization meditation", *headspace*. https://www.headspace.com/meditation/visualization. (accessed October 25, 2019).

24. Dr. Julie Connor. "7 Reasons Why It's Crucial to Have a Dream", *Dr. Julie Connor*. March 27, 2014, https://www.drjulieconnor.com/7-reasons-why-its-crucial-to-have-a-dream/. (Accessed June 16, 2019)

25. Walt Disney. "Walt Disney - All our dreams can come true, if we have the...", *BrainyQuote*.com https://www.brainyquote.com/quotes/walt_disney_163027. (accessed June 16, 2019).

26. Murielle Marie. "3 Inspiring Women Who Achieved Their Big Dreams", *Conscious Career and Business Coach. Soulful Productivity Expert. - MurielleMarie*.com https://muriellemarie.com/goals-that-matter/3-inspiring-women-who-achieved-their-big-dreams/. (accessed June 16, 2019).

27. Murielle Marie. "3 Inspiring Women Who Achieved Their Big Dreams", *Conscious Career and Business Coach. Soulful Productivity Expert. - MurielleMarie*.com https://muriellemarie.com/goals-that-matter/3-inspiring-women-who-achieved-their-big-dreams/. (accessed June 16, 2019).

28. Murielle Marie. "3 Inspiring Women Who Achieved Their Big Dreams", *Conscious Career and Business Coach. Soulful Productivity Expert. - Murielle Marie*.com https://muriellemarie.com/goals-that-matter/3-inspiring-women-who-achieved-their-big-dreams/. (accessed June 16, 2019).

Chapter 7 – TIME IS LIFE – DON'T WASTE IT

29. Harvey Mackay. "Quote by Harvey MacKay: "Time is free, but it's priceless. You can't own..."", *Goodreads*.com https://www.goodreads.com/quotes/79511-time-is-free-but-it-s-priceless-you-can-t-own-it. (accessed June 16, 2019).

30. Jim Rohn. "Jim Rohn - Time is more value than money. You can get more...", *BrainyQuote*.com https://www.brainyquote.com/quotes/jim_rohn_147516. (accessed June 16, 2019).

31. Dr. Sunday Adelaja. "6/47. WHAT DO YOU DO WITH YOUR TIME", *You-Tube 6/47*. August 21, 2016 https://www.youtube.com/watch?v=aBridLmTLTk. (accessed October 25, 2019).

32. Harmon Okinyo. "Quote by Harmon Okinyo: "Time is a currency you can only spend once, so ..."", *Goodreads*. https://www.goodreads.com/

quotes/7322221-time-is-a-currency-you-can-only-spend-once-so. (accessed June 18, 2019).

33. BBC. "Australian Open 2017: Serena Williams beats Venus Williams to set Grand Slam record", *BBC.* January 2017, https://www.bbc.com/sport/tennis/38781553. (accessed April 12, 2020).

34. Tyler O'Niel. "How Home schooling Helped Propel Simone Biles to the Olympic Gold", *PJ Media.* August 9, 2016 https://pjmedia.com/parenting/2016/08/09/how-homeschooling-helped-propel-simone-biles-to-the-olympic-gold/. (accessed June 18,2019).

Chapter 8 – A GIRL AND HER FRIENDS

35. Dr. Sunday Adelaja. Who Am I, Why am I here?" (Golden Pen Limited. 2016)

36. George Santayana. "George Santayana quotes –"One's friends are that part of the...", *BrainyQuote*.com https://www.brainyquote.com/quotes/george_santayana_105234. (accessed June 20, 2019).

37. RUTGERS.EDU – Fingerprinting in the Modern World. (accessed May 13, 2020) https://sites.rutgers.edu/fingerprinting/no-two-finger-prints-are-alike/ Rutgers.edu

38. Mary Dunbar. "Quote by Mary Dunbar: "We are each gifted in a unique and important wa..."", *Goodreads.* https://www.goodreads.com/quotes/626104-we-are-each-gifted-in-a-unique-and-important-way. (accessed June 20, 2019).

39. Suzy Kassem. "Quote by Suzy Kassem: "You were born an original work of art. Stay ori..."", *Goodreads.* https://www.goodreads.com/quotes/7393411-you-were-born-an-original-work-of-art-stay-original. (accessed June 20, 2019).

40. Raising Children Network. "Respectful romantic relationships for teenagers", *Raising Children Network.* May2, 2018 https://raisingchildren.net.au/pre-teens/communicating-relationships/romantic-relationships/respectful-relationships-for-teens.(accessed June 25, 2019).

41. Vladimir Lenin. "Vladimir Lenin Quote: Show me who your friends - Quote of Quotes", *Quote of Quotes.* https://quoteofquotes.com/vladimir-lenin-quote-show-me-who-your-friends-tell-who-you-are/. (accessed June 25, 2019).

Chapter 9 – DARE TO BE DIFFERENT

42. A. Edwards. "beautyfrosting.com", *Pinterest.* https://www.pinterest.nz/pin/419045940300321855/. (accessed June 25, 2019).

43. Sharon Marris. "https://news.sky.com/story/greta-thunberg-replies-to-critics-of-her-aspergers-being-different-is-a-superpower-" September 2, 2019. SKYNEWS.COM – (accessed May 13, 2020)

44. Anonymous. Thought Catalog. May 2, 2014 .Thoughtcatalog.

com " https://thoughtcatalog.com/anonymous/2014/05/dont-try-to-be-someone-else-youre-not-else-you-miss-out-on-who-you-truly-are/ (accessed May13, 2020)

45. Dr. Sunday Adelaja. " HOW TO BUILD YOUR SELF CONFIDENCE- SELF CONFIDENCE SERIES", *YouTube*. 4/6 May 20,2017 https://www.youtube.com/watch?v=YlZO4PTGfVU. (accessed June 30, 2019).

46. Irene Messina. "Jessica Cox is just like any other licensed pilot—except she has no arms", *Tucson Weekly*. August 2009, https://www.tucsonweekly.com/tucson/messina/Content?oid=1306035. (accessed April 12, 2020).

47. Disability Credit Canada Inc. "Famous People with Disabilities & there Quotes", *Disability Credit Canada*. November 29,2017. https://disabilitycredit-canada.com/top-16-famous-people-with-disabilities/. (accessed June 30, 2019).

48. Disability Credit Canada Inc. "Famous People with Disabilities & their Quotes", Disability Credit Canada. November 29, 2017. https://disabilitycredit-canada.com/top-16-famous-people-with-disabilities/. (accessed June 30, 2019)

49. YoungMinds. "Body image", *YoungMinds*. https://youngminds.org.uk/find-help/feelings-and-symptoms/body-image/. (accessed June 30, 2019).

50. Rebecca Flood. "BUM DEAL Model with a 59 inch bum begs doctors for help after illegal fillers injected at 'plumping parties' left her with a discoloured and lumpy bottom".*Thesun.co.uk*. May 15,2019. https://www.thesun.co.uk/fabulous/9081655/model-bum-illegal-fillers-saggy/. (accessed July 10, 2019).

51. Mind Tools Content Team. "Using Affirmations Harnessing Positive Thinking.", *Mind Tools*. https://www.mindtools.com/pages/article/affirmations.htm. (accessed July 10,2019).

Chapter 10 – MAKE A DIFFERENCE

52. Elaine S. Dalton. "Quote by Elaine S. Dalton: "If you desire to make a difference in the world...", *Goodreads*. https://www.goodreads.com/quotes/1367445-if-you-desire-to-make-a-difference-in-the-world. (accessed April 12, 2020).

53. Zuriel Oduwole. "Bio | zuriel-oduwole", *zuriel oduwole*. n.d., https://www.zurieloduwole.com/home-2. (accessed April 12, 2020).

54. Vandita. "Young Activists: 7 Teenagers Who are Truly Making a .... "July 9, 2016. AnonHQ.com https://anonhq.com/young-activists-7-teenagers-truly-making-difference-world/

55. Vandita. "Young Activists: 7 Teenagers Who are Truly Making a .... "July9, 2016. AnonHQ.com https://anonhq.com/young-activists-7-teenagers-truly-making-difference-world/

56. INDY100 FROM Independent. "11-year-old Meghan Markle wrote a letter to change a .... " December 1, 2017. Indy100.com https://www.indy100.com/article/meghan-markle-sexist-advert-letter-prince-harry-royal-engagement-suits-nottingham-wed-

ding-8086511.

57. Excellence Reporter. "Ralph Waldo Emerson: On Love, Beauty and the Purpose of Life", *Excellence Reporter*. February 18, 2019., https://excellencereporter. com/2019/02/18/ralph-waldo-emerson-on-love-beauty-and-the-purpose-of-life/. (accessed July 10, 2019).

Chapter 11 – A GIRL AND HER VALUES

58. Michelle Obama. "Michelle Obama Quotes - I have learned that as long as I hold...", *BrainyQuote.com* https://www.brainyquote.com/quotes/michelle_obama_791345. (accessed July 15, 2019).

59. Lexico.com. Powered by Oxford. Definition. Value www.lexico. com/definition/value (accessed May 13,2020)

60. Peter Marshall. "Peter Marshall Quotes - If you don't stand for something you will...", *BrainyQuote*.com https://www.brainyquote.com/quotes/peter_mar-shall_382875. (accessed July 15, 2015)

61. Elvis Presley. Elvis Presley Quotable Quotes. Goodreads.com. https://www. goodreads.com/quotes/113467-values-are-like-fingerprints-nobody-s-are-the-same-but-you. (accesses May 3, 2020)

62. Andrew Blackman. "What Are Your Personal Values? How to Define & Live by Them.". Business.tutsplus.com. August 4,2018. https://business.tutsplus. com/tutorials/what-are-personal-values--cms-31561. (accessed July 15, 2019).

63. Asmita Kadam " What are moral Values? Quora.com. August 27, 2017 https://www.quora.com/What-are-moral-values (accessed May 13,2020)

64. Nishtha Dhull. "LET'S INCULCATE MORAL VALUES.", *My Fit Brain*. https://myfitbrain.in/blog/child-psychologist/lets-inculcate-moral-values-in-kids. (accessed July 15, 2019).

65. Idowu Koyenikan. "Quote by Idowu Koyenikan: "A highly developed values system is like a comp..."", *Goodreads*. https://www.goodreads.com/quotes/7172710-a-highly-developed-values-system-is-like-a-compass-it. (accessed July 15, 2019).

66. ANSWERSDRIVE. "What are some good family values?", *AnswersDrive*. com October 2,2019, https://answersdrive.com/what-are-some-good-family-val-ues-8406386.(accessed July 15, 2019).

67. Amy Winehouse. "Amy Winehouse. - Death, Songs & Documentary – Biography", *Famous Biographies & TV Shows*. June 26, 2019. https://www.biography. com/musician/amy-winehouse. (accessed October 20, 2019).

68. Sunday Adelaja. "How to create core values in a child. How to transform small kid into big human. (2018) Golden Truth Publishing 2018.

Chapter 12 – HOW TO MAKE THE MOST OF YOUR YEARS

69. Angela Cecilia. "Quotes - Angela Cecilia (Herndon, VA) Showing 1-7 of 7", *Goodreads*. https://www.goodreads.com/quotes/list/85054726-angela-cecilia. (accessed July 20, 2019).

70. Lamentations 3:27 (New Living translations).

71. Collins Dictionary. "Self-discipline definition and meaning | Collins English", Collinsdictionary.com https://www.collinsdictionary.com/dictionary/english/self-discipline. (accessed July 20, 2019).

72. Todd Smith. "Becoming a Disciplined Person", *Little Things Matter*. February 1, 2011 http://www.littlethingsmatter.com/blog/2011/02/01/becoming-a-disciplined-person/. (accessed July 25, 2019).

73. Jim Rohn. Jim Rohn Quotes. *BrainyQuote*.com https://www.brainyquote.com/quotes/jim_rohn_132691. (accessed July 25, 2019).

74.

75. Dr. Seuss. "I can read with my eyes shut", *Goodreads*.com , https://www.goodreads.com/quotes/6806-the-more-that-you-read-the-more-things-you-will. (accessed July 25, 2019).

76. JJ Wong. "8 reasons why reading is so important.", Inspirationboost.com. July 2012. https://www.inspirationboost.com/8-reasons-why-reading-is-so-important (accessed July 25, 2019).

77. Glen Davies. "Why Is Reading Important?", Learn-to-read-prince-george.com. December, 2016 https://www.learn-to-read-prince-george.com/why-is-reading-important.html. (accessed July 25, 2019).

78. J.K Rowling. "Quotable Quote ", *Goodreads*.com https://www.goodreads.com/quotes/657790-i-do-believe-something-very-magical-can-happen-when-you. (accessed July 25, 2019).

79. Oprah Winfrey. Oprah Winfrey Quote. BrainyQuote.com https://www.brainyquote.com/quotes/oprah_winfrey_402113 (Accessed July 25, 2019).

80. Shawn Jackson "Do You Accept Responsibility for Your Actions?",.Goodchoicesgoodlife.org. 2014. http://www.goodchoicesgoodlife.org/choices-for-young-people/accepting-responsibility-/. (accessed July 26, 2019).

81. Roy T. Bennet. Famous Quotes at Quote Unquotes. Because somebody already said it best! ™ "SUCCESS - Quoteunquotes.com", https://quoteunquotes.com/success/. (accessed July 26, 2019).

82. . Shawn Jackson "Do You Accept Responsibility for Your Actions?", Goodchoicesgoodlife.org. 2014 http://www.goodchoicesgoodlife.org/choices-for-young-people/accepting-responsibility-/. (accessed July 26, 2019).

83. Oprah Winfrey. "Oprah Winfrey Quotes", *Goodreads*.com https://www.goodreads.com/quotes/585108-i-believe-luck-is-preparation-meeting-opportunity-if-you-hadn-t. (accessed July 26, 2019).

84. Ayishat Amoo. "3 Reasons why Preparation is Important", Chubmagazine.

com December 25, 2016 https://www.chubmagazine.com/2016/12/25/3-reasons-why-preparation-important/. (accessed July 26, 2019).

85. Bobby Unser. "Bobby Unser Quotes. *BrainyQuote*.com https://www.brainyquote.com/quotes/bobby_unser_126431. (accessed July 26, 2019).

86. Kevin Durant. "Quotes, Quotable Quotes", *Goodreads*. https://www.goodreads.com/quotes/699064-hard-work-beats-talent-when-talent-fails-to-work-hard. (accessed July 27, 2019).

87. Serena Williams. Serena Williams Quotes "Luck has nothing to do with it, because....", *BrainyQuote*.com https://www.brainyquote.com/quotes/serena_williams_183396. (accessed July 27, 2019).

88. Thomas Oppong. "Hard Work is The Single Greatest Competitive Advantage", Mission. org. March 15,2017 https://medium.com/the-mission/hard-work-is-the-single-greatest-competitive-advantage-8e65a1e674f4. (accessed July 27, 2019).

89. G.K Nielson. Reddit ", *Reddit.com*. 2017 https://www.reddit.com/r/quotes/comments/5d15dj/successful_people_are_not_gifted_they_just_work/. (accessed July 27, 2019).

Chapter 13 – THE PRINCIPLE OF DELAYED GRATIFICATION

90. Brian Tracy: Quotable Quotes "The ability to discipline yourself .... ", *Goodreads.com*. https://www.goodreads.com/quotes/23014. (accessed July 27, 2019).

91. Wikipedia. Gratification. March 24, 2020" https://en.wikipedia.org/wiki/Gratification" (accessed May 13, 2020)

92. Neil Patel. "The Psychology of Instant Gratification and How It Will Revolutionize Your Marketing Approach" Entreprenuer.com .June 24, 2014 https://www.entrepreneur.com/article/235088. (accessed July 30, 2019).

93. Brain Tracy. "10 Quotes About Delayed Gratification - Fiscal Fitness Phoenix", *Fiscal Fitness Phoenix*. November 11, 2015. https://fiscalfitnessphx.com/10-quotes-about-delayed-gratification/ (accessed July 30, 2019).

94. Peggy Cahn. Maturity Sayings and Quotes, *Wise Old Sayings*. http://www.wiseoldsayings.com/maturity-quotes/ (accessed January 2, 2019).

95. Ilene Strauss Cohen Ph.D. "The Benefits of Delaying Gratification", *Psychology Today*. September 20, 2019. https://www.psychologytoday.com/us/blog/your-emotional-meter/201712/the-benefits-delaying-gratification (accessed July 30, 2019).

96. Zain Asher. "Trust your struggle TEDx Euston Talk", *YouTube*. January 12, 2015. https://www.youtube.com/watch?v=BT2XlI8oeh0&t=285s. (accessed 30 July, 2019).

97. James Clear. "40 Years of Stanford Research Found That People With This One Quality Are More Likely to Succeed." https://jamesclear.com/delayed-gratification. (accessed 5 June, 2019).

98. Alykhan Gulamali. "How to Learn to Delay Gratification and Build a Great Life", Fit yourself club. November 18, 2017 https://fityourself.club/how-to-use-delayed-gratification-to-build-a-great-life-3f451302ec60. (accessed July 27, 2019).

99. Susan Gale. "Susan Gale, Quotable quotes , *Goodreads*. https://www.goodreads.com/quotes/578308-the-longer-you-have-to-wait-for-something-the-more. (accessed July 30, 2019).

Chapter 14 – SEX, DRINKS AND DRUGS

100. Unknown. "You should save the best part of yourself for the person who deserve you", *QuoteWave*. https://www.quoteswave.com/picture-quotes/69385. (accessed January 2, 2020).

101. Raising Children Network. "Teen sexuality & sexual development", *Raising Children Network*. October 18, 2019 https://raisingchildren.net.au/pre-teens/development/puberty-sexual-development/teenage-sexuality. (accessed July 30, 2019).

102. Michelle Marshall. "20 Of the Best Quotes To Empower Single Women Everywhere", *Thought Catalog*. November 20, 2017 https://thoughtcatalog.com/michelle-marshall/2017/11/20-of-the-best-quotes-to-empower-single-women-everywhere/. (accessed July 30, 2019).

103. Amy Peckham. "One Child In Every Primary School Classroom Has Received A Nude Image From An Adult", *HuffPost*. August 30, 2018. www.huffingtonpost.co.uk/entry/child-grooming. (accessed August 15, 2019).

104. ITS NOT OKAY. "Online Safety and Sexting", *ITS NOT OKAY*. http://www.itsnotokay.co.uk/children/online-safety-and-sexting/. (accessed August 15, 2019).

105. Alan Travis. The Guardian.com. "One in five women have been sexually assaulted, analysis finds" February 8, 2018. https://www.theguardian.com/uk-news/2018/feb/08/sexual-assault-women-crime-survey-england-wales-ons-police-figures (accesses May 13, 2020)

106. Raising Children Network. "Teen sexuality & sexual development", *Raising Children Network*. October 18, 2019 https://raisingchildren.net.au/pre-teens/development/puberty-sexual-development/teenage-sexuality. (accessed August 11, 2019).

107. NSPCC. "Premature sexualisation: understanding the risk", *NSPCC*. March 2011, https://www.nspcc.org.uk/globalassets/documents/information-service/seminars-premature-sexualisation-understanding-risks.pdf. (accessed August 15, 2019).

108. NSPCC. "Grooming", *NSPCC*. https://www.nspcc.org.uk/what-is-child-abuse/types-of-abuse/grooming/#what-is. (accessed August 15, 2019).

109. Helen Carter. "Rochdale child sex ring case: respected men who preyed on the vulnerable", *The Guardian*. May 2012, https://www.theguardian.com/uk/2012/may/08/rochdale-child-sex-ring-case?intcmp=239. (accessed April 12, 2020).

110. Christina Coleman. "What Happened to Kenneka Jenkins? - Essence.com", *Essence*. September12, 2017, https://www.essence.com/news/kenneka-jenkins-case-facts-what-to-know/. (accessed August 11, 2019).

111. ITS NOT OKAY. "Naomi's Story", *ITS NOT OKAY*. http://www.itsnotokay.co.uk/children/real-stories/naomis-story/. (accessed August 11, 2019).

112. Philosiblog. "Drunkenness is nothing but voluntary madness.", *Philosiblog*. March 8, 2014 https://philosiblog.com/2014/03/08/drunkenness-is-nothing-but-voluntary-madness/. (accessed August 15, 2019).

113. Nancy L. Brown. "All About Alcohol", *Sutter Health*. August 2016 https://www.sutterhealth.org/health/teens/alcohol/about-alcohol. (accessed August 20, 2019).

114. Nancy L. Brown. "All About Alcohol", *Sutterhealth*.org October 2013., https://www.sutterhealth.org/health/teens/drugs/drug-use-abuse. (accessed August 20, 2019).

115. Albert Einstein. Veeroes Quotes "If you want to live a happy life, tie it to a goal, not to people or things", Veeroesquotes.com https://veeroesquotes.com/goal-quotes-albert-einstein/. (accessed August 20, 2019).

Chapter 15 – YOU AND YOUR FAMILY RELATIONSHIPS

116. Winston S Churchill. "Winston S Churchill Quotable Quotes", Goodreads.com https://www.goodreads.com/quotes/44836-there-is-no-doubt-that-it-is-around-the-family. (accessed August 5, 2019)

117. Nancy L. Brown. "Family." *Sutter Health*. October 2013 https://www.sutterhealth.org/health/teens/relationships-social-skills/family. (accessed August 5, 2019).

118. Raising Children Network. "Good family relationships: tips & ideas", *Raising Children Network*. https://raisingchildren.net.au/grown-ups/family-life/routines-rituals-relationships/good-family-relationships. (accessed August 5, 2019).

119. Asad Meah "27-quotes-that-will-push-you-to-take-personal-responsibility-for-your-life", *AwakenTheGreatnessWithin*..com. https://www.awakenthegreatnesswithin.com/27-quotes-that-will-push-you-to-take-personal-responsibility-for-your/ (accessed August 5, 2019).

120. ENO GLOBAL Respect. May 26, 2018. https://eno-globalmedia.com/2018/05/26/respect-the-best-way-to-be-respectful-is-by-making-sure-you-are-respecting-yourself/ Eno-globalmedia.com (accessed May13, 2020)

121. Me.me. :Lessons taught by life", me.me/t/god. https://me.me/i/the-best-thing-in-life-is-that-god-sees-all-15801557. (accessed August 5, 2019)

122. Nancy L. Brown. "Improving your spirit", *Sutter Health*. October 2013 https://www.sutterhealth.org/health/teens/becoming-adult/improving-your-spirit. (accessed August 11, 2019).

123. Desmond Tutu. "Desmond Tutu quotes", *BrainyQuote*.com https://www.brainyquote.com/quotes/desmond_tutu_112366. (accessed August 5, 2019).

Chapter 16 – FINAL THOUGHTS AND ADVICE

124. Alexis Carrel. "Alexis carrel quotes ", *BrainyQuote*.com https://www.brainyquote.com/quotes/alexis_carrel_161287. (accessed. August 6, 2019).

125. Steve Maraboli: " Steve Maraboli Quotable quotes ", *Goodreads.com* . https://www.goodreads.com/quotes/319522-it-s-up-to-you-today-to-start-making-healthy-choices. (accessed August 6, 2019).

126. Imogen Dewey. "Seven things every mum should tell their teenage girl". Honey.nine.com.au 2018 https://honey.nine.com.au/mums/advice-for-teenage-girls/a1d52714-c042-4377-9c01-1a8b02c281e2. (accessed August 6, 2019).

127. Monica Torres. "11 celebrities' best advice to their younger selves", theladders.com. January 15,2018. https://www.theladders.com/career-advice/11-pieces-of-the-best-advice-that-celebrities-would-give-their-younger-selves. (accessed August 6, 2019).

128. Monica Torres. "11 celebrities' best advice to their younger selves". theladders.com. January 15, 2018 https://www.theladders.com/career-advice/11-pieces-of-the-best-advice-that-celebrities-would-give-their-younger-selves. (accessed August 6, 2019).

129. Monica Torres. "11 celebrities' best advice to their younger selves" theladders.com January 15, 2018. https://www.theladders.com/career-advice/11-pieces-of-the-best-advice-that-celebrities-would-give-their-younger-selves. (accessed August 6, 2019).

130. Lynn Andriani. "Celebs Share the Best Advice They've Ever Received or Given", *Oprah.com*. September9, 2018 http://www.oprah.com/inspiration/advice-from-celebrities/all (accessed August 10, 2019).

131. Lynn Andriani. "Celebs Share the Best Advice They've Ever Received or Given", *Oprah.com*. September 9,2018 http://www.oprah.com/inspiration/advice-from-celebrities/all. (accessed August 10, 2019).

132. Lynn Andriani. "Celebs Share the Best Advice They've Ever Received or Given", *Oprah.com September 9,2018*. http://www.oprah.com/inspiration/advice-from-celebrities/all. (accessed August 10, 2019).

133. Lynn Andriani. "Celebs Share the Best Advice They've Ever Received or Given", September 9, 2018. *Oprah.com*. http://www.oprah.com/inspiration/advice-from-celebrities/all. (accessed August 10, 2019).

134. Lydia Sweatt. SUCCESS "13 Quotes About Making Life Choices", *Success*.com October 6, 2016. https://www.success.com/13-quotes-about-making-life-choices/. (accessed August 10, 2019).

135. Rivka Hecht. International Women's day - Are women doing too much? The Times of Israel March 8 2015. https://blogs.timesofisrael.com/international-al-womens-day-are-women-doing-too-much/ (accessed May 15, 2020)

136. Kavita Ramdas. "Heart of a Warrior Woman", *Heart of a Warrior Woman.* https://www.heartofawarriorwoman.com/ (accessed August 11, 2019).

137. Lorna, Jane Clarkson. December 11, 2016 https://www.instagram.com/p/BN48AZAB0VE/?taken-by=ljclarkson. (accessed January 2, 2020).

138. Coco Channel. AZQUOTES. Coco Channel quotes. https://www.azquotes.com/quote/855795 (accessed August 11, 2019).

Printed in Great Britain
by Amazon